OCCASIONAL PAPER

How Goes the "War on Drugs"?

An Assessment of U.S. Drug Problems and Policy

Jonathan P. Caulkins, Peter Reuter,
Martin Y. Iguchi, James Chiesa

Prepared for The Ford Foundation

RAND Drug Policy Research Center

A JOINT ENDEAVOR WITHIN RAND HEALTH
AND RAND INFRASTRUCTURE, SAFETY, AND ENVIRONMENT

The research described in this report was supported by core RAND Drug Policy Research Center (DPRC) funds provided by The Ford Foundation. The DPRC is co-administered by two research units of the RAND Corporation, RAND Health, and RAND Infrastructure, Safety, and Environment (ISE).

Library of Congress Cataloging-in-Publication Data

How goes the "war on drugs"? : an assessment of U.S. drug programs and policy / Jonathan P. Caulkins ... [et al.].
p. cm.
"OP-121."
Includes bibliographical references.
ISBN 0-8330-3737-4 (pbk. : alk. paper)
1. Narcotics, Control of—United States—Evaluation. 2. Drug abuse—United States—Prevention—Evaluation. I. Caulkins, Jonathan P. (Jonathan Paul), 1965– II. Rand Corporation. III. Series: Occasional paper (Rand Corporation) ; 121.

HV5825.H68 2005
363.45'0973—dc22

2004029770

Published 2005 by the RAND Corporation
1776 Main Street, P.O. Box 2138, Santa Monica, CA 90407-2138
1200 South Hayes Street, Arlington, VA 22202-5050
201 North Craig Street, Suite 202, Pittsburgh, PA 15213-1516
RAND URL: http://www.rand.org/
To order RAND documents or to obtain additional information, contact
Distribution Services: Telephone: (310) 451-7002;
Fax: (310) 451-6915; Email: order@rand.org

Preface

For the past 15 years, the RAND Corporation's Drug Policy Research Center (DPRC) has been analyzing trends in drug use and consequences in the United States and evaluating policies intended to respond to drug-related problems. Focus is essential if research is to be successful, so each of our efforts to date has necessarily addressed only aspects, often fairly narrow aspects, of the drug problem and policy spectrum. We thought it might be helpful to policymakers and the general public if we stood back, took a broader view, and attempted to synthesize some of the findings of our own research and that of others. It seemed to us that there might be some interest in a concise, accessible, objective view of where the United States has been, now stands, and is going in its long "war on drugs." We are not the first to attempt such a synthesis, but other volumes have been lengthy or written to support a certain policy agenda (typically either the prevailing government policy or a dramatically differing alternative).

We begin by assessing the success of drug policies to date and then review possible reasons why they have not been more successful. We consider the drug war's "collateral damage" and attempt to understand why alternative policies have not been tried. Finally, we lay out some possible futures for drug problems and policy in the United States and infer from our review of evidence some broad suggestions for a healthier policy mix and debate.

We cannot, of course, be encyclopedic in a small space; various interesting topics and perspectives must be omitted. While we have tried to account for different viewpoints, this review inevitably reflects the particular analytic interests of the DPRC. For those interested in learning more, we append a list of books that go into more detail but that should still be accessible to the educated layperson.

Footnotes to the text provide sources for the factual statements made and for some of the hypotheses and arguments where these have been previously set out in a compelling fashion, as well as technical elaboration on some of the text points. We do not attempt a comprehensive list of sources for each point and, in being selective, we sometimes list a recent, readily available source rather than an original one.

To enhance readability of the text, references in the text are given only at the ends of paragraphs. Where a source applies only to a specific point within the paragraph (as is typically the case), that is so indicated in the footnote. Sources for statements repeated in the text are not repeated. Most citations are abbreviated; for the full citation, see the reference list at the end. The preparation of this Occasional Paper was supported by core DPRC funds provided by The Ford Foundation. The DPRC is coadministered by two research units of the RAND Corporation, RAND Health and RAND Infrastructure, Safety, and Environment (ISE).

Contents

Figures

Abbreviations

DPRC	Drug Policy Research Center
HCV	hepatitis C virus
NCHS	National Center for Health Statistics
NHSDA	National Household Survey on Drug Abuse
NIDA	National Institute on Drug Abuse
NSDUH	National Survey on Drug Use and Health
ONDCP	Office of National Drug Control Policy
R&D	research and development
SAMHSA	Substance Abuse and Mental Health Services Administration

CHAPTER ONE

Introduction

Illegal drugs are a $60-billion-per-year industry patronized by at least 16 million Americans, 7 percent of the U.S. population over the age of 12. This level of usage clearly worries the rest of the population: From 1985 until 2001, "drugs" was consistently 1 of the top 10 answers when Americans were asked what they thought was the most important problem facing the nation.[1]

In response to such concerns, federal and state legislators and executive-branch officials have enacted and implemented policies that, while diverse in approach, are oriented toward enforcement. These policies include the prohibition of almost any use or possession of cocaine, heroin, marijuana, and a wide variety of other psychoactive substances. To make it more difficult to buy such drugs, strategies have been implemented that range from eradication of crops like coca in source countries, through interdiction of smugglers, to disruption of street markets and incarceration of dealers within U.S. borders. At thc same time, governmental agencies have sought to reduce Americans' demand for drugs through treatment of substance abusers and prevention programs offered through schools and over the media. However, most expenditures on drug control at federal, state, and local levels combined have been directed to enforcement.[2]

Over the past 15 years, these measures have had a dramatic impact on some segments of society. They have not, however, led to substantial decreases in the severity of America's drug-

---

[1] Use data are for any illicit drug in the 30 days prior to survey, from pp. 21–22 of "Data Supplement" (available only online at http://www.whitehousedrugpolicy.gov/publications/policy/ndcs03/drug_related_data.pdf), The White House, *National Drug Control Strategy,* Office of National Drug Control Policy, Washington, D.C., February 2003, citing Substance Abuse and Mental Health Services Administration, *National Household Survey on Drug Abuse.* The survey, renamed the *National Survey on Drug Use and Health* in 2002, annually measures the prevalence of drug and alcohol use among household members aged 12 and over; because it undersamples the homeless and ignores the institutionalized, it misses many frequent users of expensive and addictive drugs. Because of that and because it relies on self-reports of illegal activity, its estimates are known to be conservative (see Manski, Pepper, and Petrie, eds., *Informing America's Policy on Illegal Drugs,* pp. 78–79, 87–88). Polling data from various organizations, 1985–2002, are from the LexisNexis Web site, reported by the Roper Center at the University of Connecticut, "Public Opinion Online."

[2] MacCoun and Reuter, *Drug War Heresies,* Chapter 2.

related problems, prompting strident denunciations of current policy. Many critics argue that the increased toughness of that policy has done more harm than good. Some go so far as to suggest that drugs should simply be legalized. Such attacks have induced equally strong defenses of current policy by enforcement proponents, who believe that failure of the patient to improve is an indicator that even stronger medicine is required. They also fear that watering down the regimen will surrender what gains have been made to date.[3]

Evidence is typically lost in this debate. What evidence makes its way to the surface is often cited selectively to make a case for a preferred position. Here, we attempt to sort through and weigh the evidence to see where it takes us and what kind of story it tells about updated progress and options for the future in the "war on drugs."[4]

Evidence is not the whole story, of course. Evidence has little bearing on the kind of moral beliefs many people hold: that the use of psychoactive drugs is wrong, and their sale more wrong; or that government intrusion into the drug use decision is wrong, and harsh sanctions against possession are also wrong. While we acknowledge such concerns, particularly as they play out in the political arena, empirical evidence per se can shed no light on them. However, the evidence should be of interest even to those primarily motivated by morality and a sense of justice. After all, moral concerns can conflict, and the evidence may suggest unintended consequences of morally driven decisions.[5]

In this paper, we are interested primarily in choices at the strategic level—choices, for example, among strict prohibition, moderate prohibition, or decriminalization; choices among goals, for example, those focusing on use reduction or those focusing on harm reduction; decisions as to the appropriate roles of supply and demand control. We do not try to deal with questions of how a strategy is to be implemented once it has been selected. These include issues such as how to design a prevention or treatment intervention or whether treatment program A is better than program B. There is no question that such issues are very important, because there is enormous variation in effectiveness across programs and, hence, enormous potential for a good strategy to get undermined by poor tactics and implementation. The focus here, however, is on information that will give readers a better understanding of big-picture, strategic themes.[6]

---

[3] For societal impacts, see "What about Bonuses and Collateral Damage?" below. For trends in drug-related problems, see "Has the War Achieved Its Goals?" below. On drug legalization, see, for example, Cussen and Block, "Legalize Drugs Now!: An Analysis of the Benefits of Legalized Drugs."

[4] An example of selective citation is the assertion by Cussen and Block in "Legalize Drugs Now!" that drug quantities consumed do not respond much to price changes, which ignores evidence to the contrary; see, for example, Caulkins et al., *Mandatory Minimum Drug Sentences*, pp. 84–85.

[5] On morality as an evidence-discouraging factor, see Reuter, "Why Does Research Have So Little Impact on American Drug Policy?"

[6] On variation in treatment program effectiveness, see Duhamel, "Drug Use Outcomes in Four Substance Abuse Treatment Studies," citing Dean Gerstein and Robert Johnson, *Prospective and Retrospective Studies of Substance Abuse Treatment Outcomes: Methods and Results of Four Large-Scale Follow-Up Programs,* National Evaluation Data Services, 1999; however, see caution in Chapter Three, Note 4. On variation in prevention program effectiveness, see Caulkins et al., *School-Based Drug Prevention,* pp. 61–62.

CHAPTER TWO

How Successful Has the War on Drugs Been?

The first response to this question ought not to be an answer but another question: Successful at achieving what goals? What is the drug war supposed to be accomplishing?

Before answering this question, we should make three points. First, drug control rhetoric has sometimes included references to a "drug-free society." By this standard, of course, U.S. policy on drugs has been a failure and so will always be. No modern democratic state has been drug-free, and America will not be the first. Thus, it is not reasonable to require that the war on drugs eliminate drug use to be regarded as successful. (Whether the drug-free society has rhetorical value as an idealistic goal is another matter. It could be argued that if the goal were not so ambitious, the campaign would achieve even less. Conversely, unrealistic goals may serve as the rationale for policies that will then also fail at achieving more practical objectives.)[1]

Second, "war" is not an apt metaphor when identified with policy seeking to control drug use. We use it here because it still enjoys some currency in the popular press and it is a convenient way of referring to the prevailing set of policies emphasizing enforcement. However, the campaign against drugs includes the expenditure of substantial sums on such non-war-like activities as drug abuse treatment and prevention. Thus, the "drug war" metaphor has fallen out of favor even among those most comfortable with the current enforcement-focused approach. Our use of the term is for convenience and should be understood in this context.

Third, America's drug use problem extends beyond drugs whose use by almost anyone is illegal, for example, cocaine, heroin, and marijuana. Adult abuse of alcohol, underage use of alcohol and tobacco, and illicit use of prescription drugs all carry addiction risk and burden

[1] Examples of recent references to freedom from drugs include Pres. William J. Clinton, " … move us closer to a drug-free America," from The White House, "The President's Message," *The National Drug Control Strategy: 1999,* p. iii; Pres. George W. Bush, " … setting our Nation on the road to a drug-free society," from President, Proclamation, "Proclamation 7470—Family Day, 2001," p. 1370; and Sen. Patrick Leahy, " … our shared goal of a drug-free America," *Congressional Record—Senate,* December 5, 2001.

society with economic and health costs. In fact, it has been estimated that the costs of tobacco use alone exceed those of all the illegal drugs combined. However, "drugs" as a social problem and the "war on drugs" as a solution are both typically interpreted as applying only to the generally illegal drugs. In fact, the current use reduction goals of the national drug strategy explicitly exclude adolescent alcohol and tobacco use. Therefore, we restrict ourselves here to drugs whose use is inherently illicit in the United States.[2]

What Have the Goals Been?

The goals of national drug control strategy have varied to a minor extent, since the first annual strategy volume was issued in 1989. That initial version focused on reducing the overall level of drug use, as well as reducing initiation and use at every level of intensity from that of casual users to that of addicts. Other official objectives included reductions in hospital emergency department mentions of drug-associated admissions (a measure of harm to users); in the import, availability, and domestic production of drugs; and in adolescents' approval of drug use.[3]

Over the course of the 1990s, the goals were simplified to the reduction of drug use and drug-related consequences. The current administration's strategy places the emphasis on measures of use alone. It sets two two-year goals: a 10 percent reduction in current use by adolescents (relative to use in 2000–2001) and the same for adults (relative to use in 2002). Two analogous five-year goals seek 25 percent reductions. "Current use" means the percentage of the population reporting any use of an illicit drug within the previous month, as documented by the Monitoring the Future survey (for adolescents) and the National Survey on Drug Use and Health (for adults). The two-year 10-percent goals match those of the original 1989 strategy, while the five-year 25-percent goals replace the 10-year 25-percent goals of the original strategy. The current strategy also characterizes education, treatment, and market disruption as national priorities.[4]

The current national drug control strategy appears motivated by a desire to reduce the adverse consequences of drug use. However, there are no explicit goals associated with reducing such important consequences as overdoses, lost productivity, and HIV infection. This partly reflects the difficulty in accounting for progress against broader objectives. There are few drug-related outcomes for which even moderately plausible measures are available. For example, there has never been a credible estimate of U.S. marijuana production, and estimates of the number of persons addicted to heroin or cocaine have been subject to large revisions every two or three years. The percentage of individuals (addicted or not) recently using any drug is one of the very few transparent and moderately credible measures available.[5]

---

[2] Comparative social cost estimates are based on results given by Caulkins et al., *School-Based Drug Prevention,* p. 21. Current national strategy is from The White House, *National Drug Control Strategy,* February 2003, p. 4.

[3] The White House, *National Drug Control Strategy,* February 1989, pp. 94–97.

[4] The White House, *National Drug Control Strategy,* March 2004, http://www.whitehousedrugpolicy.gov/publications/policy/ndcs04/intro.html.

[5] A consequence-oriented motivation for the national strategy can be inferred from passages in The White House, "Healing America's Drug Users: Getting Treatment Resources Where They Are Needed," *National Drug Control Strategy,* March 2004,

The national strategy's hopes for consequence reduction thus rest on the reasonable expectation that lower use will lead to fewer adverse consequences. However, most persons responding "yes" to questions about current use are light users, whereas adverse consequences are more closely associated with heavy use. Thus, progress measured toward a use reduction goal will not necessarily reflect progress toward consequence reduction. Reduction of casual marijuana use by a certain percentage will not reduce drug use consequences nearly as much as reduction of heavy cocaine use by the same percentage. A consequence reduction goal might thus imply an allocation of control effort (e.g., a cocaine focus) differing from that implied by use reduction (e.g., a marijuana focus, because there are so many more marijuana users than cocaine users).[6]

Has the War Achieved Its Goals?

Measured against its goals, early and more recent, the drug war has had a mixed record, at least superficially. The percentage of the population reporting past-month use of some illicit drug declined by half between 1985 and 1992. While drug use by that measure is up by about a third since then, meaningful decreases in the number of cocaine users continued through the mid-1990s (see Figure 2.1). Since 1990 the number of frequent users of cocaine (and of heroin) has declined modestly, according to official estimates. Such trends might be read as reflecting success in getting users to quit or in keeping prospective users from starting, or both. However, keeping kids from starting drugs is separately measured, and initiation of marijuana, cocaine, and hallucinogens went up in the 1990s and has stayed there. Furthermore, current use of marijuana by teenagers increased substantially in the mid- to late 1990s (see Figure 2.2); in 2003, 21 percent of 12th-graders reported having used marijuana or hashish within the previous month. And total drug consumption does not always follow the number of users. In the 1980s, for example, the number of cocaine users fell, but the quantity consumed stayed the same, as heavy users accounted for a larger fraction of the user population. Not coincidentally,

---

http://www.whitehousedrugpolicy.gov/publications/policy/ndcs04/healing_amer.html. Regarding the volatility of addiction estimates, in 2000 the Office of National Drug Control Policy (ONDCP) estimated that in 1997 there were 3.5 million chronic cocaine users; one year later the estimate for 1997 was revised to 2.85 million. In the same reports the number of chronic heroin users for 1992 was revised upward from 630,000 to 955,000. Data are from Abt Associates, Inc., (Rhodes, Layne, Johnston, and Hozik), *What America's Users Spend on Illegal Drugs, 1988–1998,* December 2000, p. 10, and Abt Associates, Inc., *What America's Users Spend on Illegal Drugs, 1988–2000,* December 2001, p. 9.

[6] According to SAMHSA, *National Household Survey on Drug Use and Health,* 2003, 75 percent of household members using cocaine within the past year used it fewer than 50 times, for an average of once a week. Users of other drugs followed suit: most reported using fewer than 50 times. National Survey on Drug Use and Health (NSDUH) data are at http://oas.samhsa.gov/nhsda/2k3tabs/PDF/Sect7peTabs1to12.pdf. We call use rates less frequent than once a week "light use" in accordance with Everingham and Rydell, *Modeling the Demand for Cocaine,* p. 14. As to the preponderance of heavy use in giving rise to adverse consequences, we rely on the proportionality of social costs to grams of drug consumed, and on the preponderance of heavy use in grams consumed. The first is from Caulkins et al., *School-Based Drug Prevention,* pp. 19–21, the second from Everingham and Rydell, *Modeling the Demand for Cocaine,* pp. 47–49, who show that in 1992, when light users were over 75 percent of all cocaine users, heavy users accounted for most of the consumption. Variations in the consequences of light marijuana versus heavy cocaine use are from Caulkins et al., *School-Based Drug Prevention,* p. 21.

Figure 2.1
Use of Marijuana and Cocaine Have Fallen in the Past 20 Years

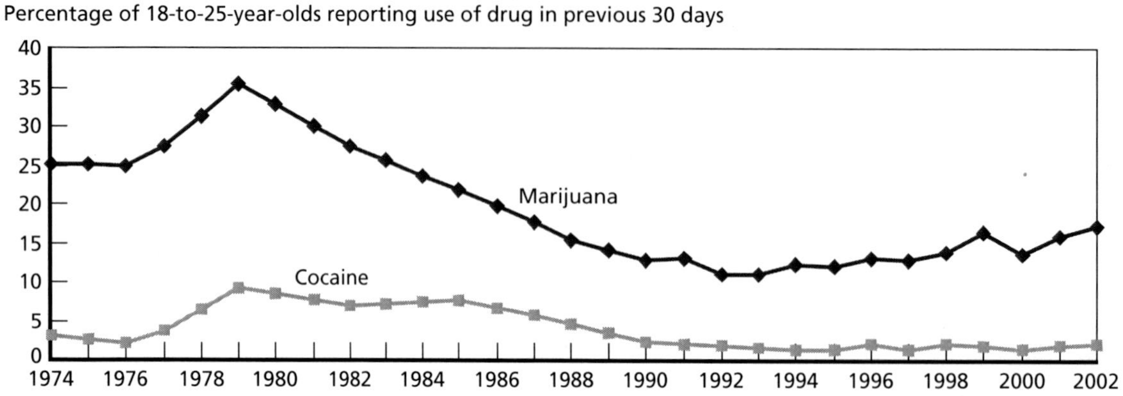

RAND *OP121-1*

SOURCE: Data are from the National Institute on Drug Abuse (NIDA) and Substance Abuse and Mental Health Services Administration (SAHMSA), National Household Survey on Drug Abuse, and SAMHSA, "2003 National Survey on Drug Use and Health: Detailed Tables," Table 1.3B, http://oas.samhsa.gov/nhsda/2k3tabs/PDF/Sect1peTabs1to18.pdf. Data for 1975, 1978, 1980, 1981, 1983, 1984, 1986, 1987, and 1989 are interpolated. Data after 1999 are not strictly comparable to those from earlier years because of technical changes in survey method.

Figure 2.2
Use of Marijuana by High School Seniors Has Increased

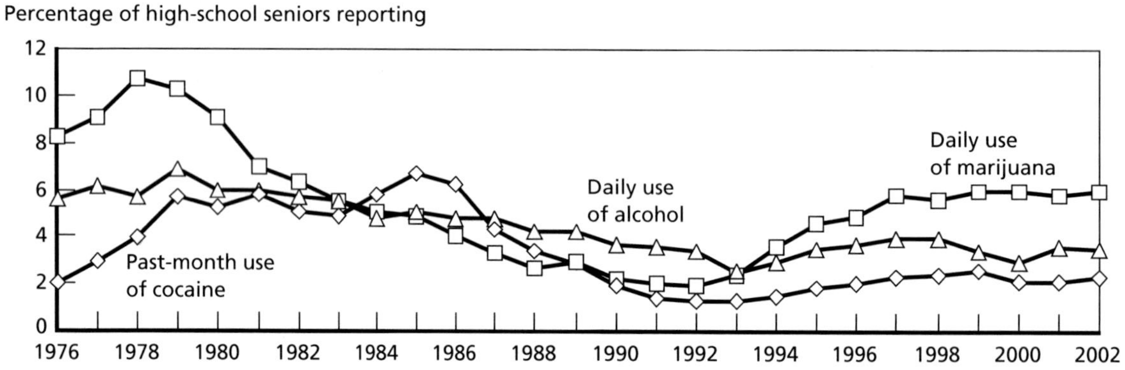

RAND *OP121-2*

SOURCE: Data are from "Monitoring the Future: 2003 Data from In-School Surveys of 8th-, 10th, and 12th-Grade Students," http://www.monitoringthefuture.org/data/03data.html#2003data-drugs, Tables 6 and 7 ("Long-Term Trends"). Monitoring the Future, administered by the University of Michigan, annually examines drug-related issues, including recency of drug use, perceived harmfulness of drugs, disapproval of drug use, and perceived availability of drugs among 8th, 10th, and 12th graders (see p. 5 of "Data Supplement" to *National Drug Control Strategy,* 2003); again, self-reports of illegal activity and omission of a potential high-use group (in this case, drop-outs) bias the estimates toward conservatism (see Manski, Pepper, and Petrie, *Informing America's Policy on Illegal Drugs,* pp. 79, 82–84, 87–88).

ill effects on users, as indicated by drug-related ER admissions, were either steady or rising (see Figure 2.3).[7]

Further indicators of the effectiveness (or lack thereof) of the prevailing policy can be found in measures associated with the drug supply pipeline and markets. Some such measures, such as the amount of drugs seized, are too gross to be meaningful. If more drugs are seized this year than last year, does that mean that more drugs are being removed from U.S. streets or that more drugs are being sent? Measures of drug prices (and availability on the street) are more helpful. That is because a principal objective of drug control is to constrain supply sufficiently to reduce availability and drive up price, making drug use less attractive. The price record suggests that supply control efforts have failed to much reduce the use of any established drug. Retail cocaine prices have from time to time been responsive to more intensified efforts to interdict smugglers, but they have soon fallen again, presumably because smugglers have discovered new routes or other ways to circumvent interdiction. The overall trend in cocaine and heroin retail prices during most of the past two decades has been downward (after adjusting for potency). That suggests *greater* availability of drugs on the street in the United States, not less. Greater availability and lower price are likely to have made use cheaper and more attractive, thus taking some of the pressure off users to quit or scale back and making it easier for youths to initiate. Nonetheless, estimated cocaine consumption has fallen in recent years, while heroin consumption may have risen. At the same time, no fourth drug has yet grown in consequence and popularity to join the "big three" of cocaine, heroin, and marijuana. Every year or two a new drug threatens to be the "new crack," and methamphetamines may indeed grow to become one of the "big four," but the vast majority of the scores of illicit drugs have a very small market share. It has been estimated that in 1999, Americans spent $36 billion on cocaine, $11 billion on heroin, $10 billion on marijuana, $5.8 billion on methamphetamines, and $2.6 billion on all other illegal drugs combined (see Figure 2.4).[8]

---

[7] Percentages reporting past-month use of any illicit drug are from p. 21 of "Data Supplement" to The White House, *National Drug Control Strategy,* 2003, citing National Institute for Drug Abuse (NIDA) and Substance Abuse and Mental Health Services Administration (SAMHSA), *National Household Survey on Drug Abuse;* number of frequent users is from "Data Supplement," The White House, *National Drug Control Strategy,* Table 3; adolescent initiation rates are from Substance Abuse and Mental Health Services Administration, Office of Applied Studies, *2003 National Survey on Drug Use & Health: Detailed Tables,* http://oas.samhsa.gov/nhsda/2k3tabs/PDF/Sect4peTabs1to14.pdf, Tables 4.1A, 4.2A, and 4.5A; 12th-grader marijuana or hashish use is from "Monitoring the Future: 2003 Data from In-School Surveys of 8th-, 10th-, and 12th-Grade Students," http://www.monitoringthefuture.org/data/03data.html#2003data-drugs, Table 2. Total cocaine consumption trend is from Everingham and Rydell, *Modeling the Demand for Cocaine,* p. 49. Emergency department mentions are from NIDA and SAMHSA, *Drug Abuse Warning Network,* 2002.

[8] For more on enforcement's effect on the market, see Rydell and Everingham, *Controlling Cocaine* pp. 9–15, and The White House, *National Drug Control Strategy,* February 2002, p. 21. For a study favoring the effect of interdiction on cocaine prices, see Crane, Rivolo, and Comfort, *An Empirical Examination of Counterdrug Interdiction Program Effectiveness,* pp. IV-1 to IV-7. For smuggler adaptation, see Reuter, Crawford, and Cave, *Sealing the Borders: The Effects of Increased Military Participation in Drug Intervention,* pp. 33–35. Overall price trends are from Caulkins, "Measurement and Analysis of Drug Problems and Drug Control Efforts," in David Duffee, ed., *Measurement and Analysis of Crime and Justice,* pp. 391–449. Cocaine and heroin consumption and total expenditures on drugs are from Abt Associates, Inc., *What America's Users Spend on Illegal Drugs, 1988–2000,* pp. 19 and 31.

Figure 2.3
ER Mentions Have Been Increasing

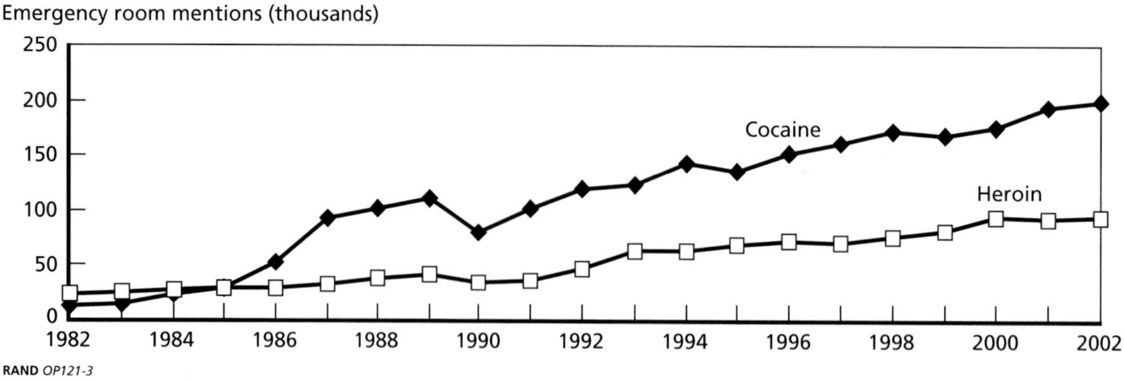

SOURCE: Data are from NIDA and SAMHSA, *Drug Abuse Warning Network,* for example, "Emergency Department Trends from DAWN," Table 2.1.0, at http://dawninfo.samhsa.gov/pubs_94_02/edpubs/2002final/#publishedtables. Data from 1994 on have been recalculated by SAMHSA and are not strictly comparable with earlier numbers (according to p. 42 of "Data Supplement" to *National Drug Control Strategy*, 2003). The Drug Abuse Warning Network provides data from medical examiners on drug-related deaths and from hospital emergency departments on drug-related episodes by type of drug, reason for taking it, demographic characteristics of the user, and metropolitan area. (See p. 8 of "Data Supplement.")

Figure 2.4
A Few Substances Dominate the Illegal-Drug Market

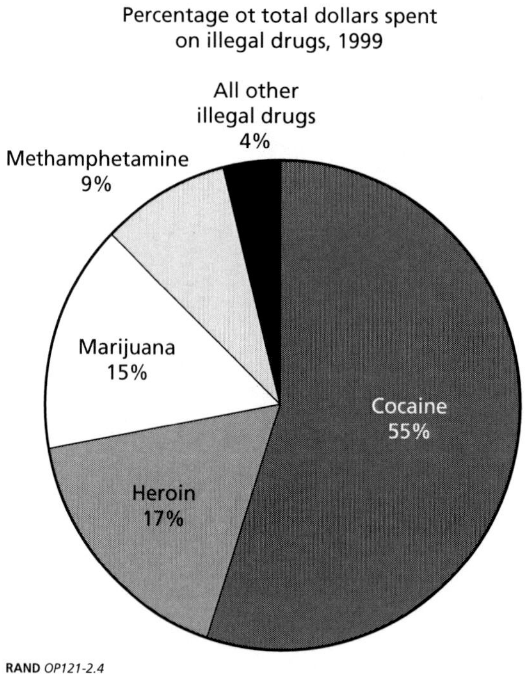

What Other Factors Need to Be Taken into Account?

We said that *superficially*, the drug war's record has been mixed. We say *superficially* because so far, we have been discussing drug use and effect trends as if the only thing that influenced them were government control policy. Actually, drug prices and demand vary over time in response to numerous factors unrelated to government action, just as the price of, and demand for, other goods vary. For example, *national* trends in the use of any drug are an aggregation of *individual* use patterns, which are influenced by a panoply of social, cultural, and biological factors. The superficial record of drug problem indicators might thus understate (or overstate) the effectiveness of government policy, depending on trends in individual preferences and the social and cultural context.

The following pages address some of the factors that make it imprudent to assume that trends in drug problems one way or the other reflect solely the effectiveness or ineffectiveness of government policy. We describe the patterns into which individual use falls and the national drug epidemics into which individual use "careers" aggregate. We also attempt to afford some perspective on the relatively narrow scope of recent U.S. drug problems and policy by briefly summarizing some broader geographic and historical variations.

"Careers" of Individual Users

Most users of any drug begin using it in their teen or young adult years. The single most important factor promoting drug use is whether family or friends engage in it. People are not, of course, slaves to their acquaintances. They may have an underlying predilection, possibly a genetic one, toward drug use or not, and they have an ability to "say no," although some people are more suggestible than others. Nonetheless, social contacts play a key role in the initiation of drug use.[9]

The course of drug use plays out differently in different people. Most people who try any drug, even heroin, use it only experimentally or continue use moderately and without ill effect. The problem (among others) with drug use is not that it *will* inevitably lead to addiction but that it *can* lead to addiction. Some fraction of people who begin using any drug move on to heavy use of that drug, with all the ill consequences specific to that drug that heavy use entails. How big a fraction of experimenters or casual users become heavy users? It has been estimated that 23 percent of those who try heroin, 17 percent of those who try cocaine, and 9 percent of those who try marijuana become clinically dependent on the drug (the rates for tobacco and alcohol are 32 percent and 15 percent, respectively).[10]

It is the heavy users that represent a true burden on society, because, while heavy users are only a minority of those who ever try a drug, their "use careers" last longer. Thus, heavy users represent a larger fraction of those using a drug at any given time than of those who ever try it. And because they use at higher rates, heavy users represent a larger fraction of total consumption. In fact, the average heavy user of cocaine uses 25 times as much of the drug in his or her lifetime as the average person who consumes cocaine for some period of time but never turns to heavy use. Heavy users' higher consumption levels also make them more liable to require

---

[9] The NSDUH asks current and former drug users their age of initiation, allowing derivation of a mean age of initiation for each year back into the 1960s. For the 1970s and 1980s, that mean ranged as follows: marijuana, 18 to 19; cocaine, 19 to 23; heroin, 19 to 25; hallucinogens, 18 to 20; methamphetamines, 18 to 22. Data are from Substance Abuse and Mental Health Services Administration, Office of Applied Studies, *2003 National Survey on Drug Use & Health: Detailed Tables,* http://oas.samhsa.gov/nhsda/2k3tabs/PDF/Sect4peTabs1to14.pdf, Tables 4.1A, 4.2A, 4.4A, 4.5A, and 4.13A, citing the 2002 and 2003 NSDUHs. We omit the 1990s because younger respondents could not have initiated as older adults during those years, thus biasing the means downwards. "The single most important factor" is from Botvin, "Principles of Prevention." On the role of genes in drug use, see Vanyukov and Tarter, "Genetic Studies of Substance Abuse."

[10] Clinical dependence rates are from Anthony, Warner, and Kessler, "Comparative Epidemiology of Dependence on Tobacco, Alcohol, Controlled Substances, and Inhalants."

health care and more likely to turn to crime to support their habit. They are the primary source of drug market revenues, which themselves constitute a social problem. Most drug-related violence is the result of attempts to control the wealth flowing through the cocaine and heroin markets—wealth that attracts young people to criminal careers. It has been estimated, for example, that almost two-thirds of the drug-related homicides in the United States are market-related, as opposed to murders committed "under the influence" or for the purpose of supporting the killer's drug habit, as during a robbery.[11]

For some consumers, heavy use is the final resting place, literally: many heroin users continue use until their (often early) death. A long-term study of heroin addicts found that, after 33 years, 11 percent of the original subjects had died of a drug overdose, 7 percent of chronic liver disease, and 10 percent from homicides, suicides, or accidents. Altogether, 49 percent of the original sample had died after 33 years (their average age at the start of the study was 25). Of those interviewed at 33 years (42 percent of the original sample), fewer than half had been abstinent for more than 5 years; 27 percent of those not in prison and willing to be tested showed positive urinalyses at the time. The average reported heroin-using career was 30 years.[12]

It is thus important in interpreting drug use data to keep in mind that people start using drugs and (some heroin users excepted) stop doing so, with varying lengths and intensities of use in between. These behaviors may be heavily, partly, or not at all influenced by government policy.

Just as there is a risk that a casual drug user will become addicted, so is there a risk that a tobacco or alcohol user will become a marijuana user. Marijuana users run a risk of moving on to one of the expensive drugs like cocaine, heroin, or methamphetamines. Again, while there is a risk, this does not *typically* happen (and the relationship is not necessarily causal, a point we will take up shortly). Many of those who do start using a new drug do so without abandoning their previous one. Heavy users are thus often polydrug users.[13]

The drug to which a user turns next can be influenced by price, and prices, as we have seen, can move independently of government action. But a falling price for one drug does not mean that users will switch to that drug and quit using another. They could use more of both, if the

---

[11] As of 1992, the annual exit rates from light cocaine use were estimated at 0.15 to nonuse and 0.024 to heavy use, implying a use career of 1/(0.15 + 0.024) or 5.75 years. The exit rates from heavy use were estimated at 0.04 to light use and 0.02 to nonuse, implying a use career of 17 years (exit rates are from Everingham and Rydell, *Modeling the Demand for Cocaine,* p. 17). Preponderance of heavy use in current use is from Everingham and Rydell, pp. 14–17. Lifetime consumption ratio can be calculated from the ratio of heavy users' annual consumption to that of light users, 8.25 (inverting the calculation in Everingham and Rydell, p. 17), and the user careers estimated above. Because heavy users are assumed to have a light-use career first, heavy users consume at the light-use rate for 5.75 years and at 8.25 times the light-use rate for 17 years, so the lifetime ratio is then [5.75 + (8.25 x 17)]/5.75 = 25. Source of drug-related violence is from Caulkins et al., *Mandatory Minimum Drug Sentences,* pp. 68, 175–183.

[12] Hser et al., "A 33-Year Follow-Up of Narcotics Addicts."

[13] More specifically, there is a much higher probability that a cigarette or alcohol user will become a marijuana user than that a nonuser of cigarettes or alcohol will, and analogously for marijuana use as a precursor to cocaine and other illicit-drug use. These relationships are from The National Center on Addiction and Substance Abuse at Columbia University, *Cigarettes, Alcohol, Marijuana,* pp. 9–16. However, these probabilities have been falling among the post-1963 birth cohorts (Golub and Johnson, "Variation in Youthful Risks of Progression from Alcohol and Tobacco to Marijuana and to Hard Drugs Across Generations," pp. 225–32). Forty-four percent of amphetamine (including methamphetamine) users reported as entering treatment in 2001 acknowledged using marijuana also, as did 31 percent of crack users (SAMHSA, Office of Applied Studies, *Treatment Episode Data Set (TEDS): 1992–2001,* Chapter 3, also at http://www.dasis.samhsa.gov/teds01/teds2k1chp3.htm; note "users" here are actually treatment episodes, that is, the same user may be counted twice or more).

two are attractive to use in combination. In fact, data on price and use suggest that marijuana, cocaine, and heroin are, if anything, complements, that is, an increase in the use of any of them (e.g., because of a decrease in price) is accompanied by an increase in use of the others.[14]

While there is no doubt that some users move from one drug to another, it is not clear that use of one drug "causes" or even encourages use of others. In particular, use of marijuana has been called a gateway to other drug use, the notion being that marijuana use increases the likelihood of using more dangerous drugs like cocaine or heroin. This notion is at least plausible: users' appetites for other drug experiences *might* be whetted by pleasurable use of marijuana. The gateway hypothesis also appears to draw support from the fact that marijuana users are many times more likely to become hard-drug users than are people who do not use marijuana. Furthermore, people who use marijuana and hard drugs at one point or another almost invariably use marijuana first. However, such evidence is not by itself sufficient to support a causal relationship between marijuana and other drug use. It has been shown that the apparent elevation in risk of hard-drug use among marijuana users could also be explained by two factors in combination: differences in opportunities to use various drugs (marijuana is more readily available to young people than hard drugs) and the possibility that individuals differ in their propensities to try *any* drugs. This alternative explanation has been partially undermined by further empirical work on twins showing that in genetically identical or very similar individuals, marijuana use is indeed associated with a higher probability of other drug use. The question of marijuana's gateway status has thus not been settled. It is noteworthy that marijuana's inferred gateway effect is a linchpin of the argument for differentiating marijuana control policy from alcohol control (although an argument can be made that alcohol might also be a gateway drug).[15]

Epidemics and Control Policy

Because drug use is spread mainly through social contacts and because most users sooner or later desist from use, patterns of drug use over time can have some of the characteristics of a contagious epidemic. Interest in cocaine, for example, was revitalized in the 1970s, spread rapidly through the mid-1980s, and then began subsiding. In cocaine's case, enforcement may have played a role in the recession of the "epidemic," but the epidemic pattern has held for different drugs in diverse countries with varying control policies in different eras. It is evident that factors other than government policies are at work. The increases in drug use at the "outbreak" of an epidemic are also far faster than corresponding changes in underlying social variables (e.g., unemployment). The likely cause is that, while the epidemic is in outbreak mode, large numbers of new, light users are recruiting even larger numbers of light users. With the passage of time and the progression of more consumers to heavy use, adverse effects become more noticeable and some of the sheen begins to wear off the drug. Light use, with its risk of addiction and ill effects, no longer seems so attractive, and that dilutes the recruiting power of light users. Furthermore, as social circles amenable to drug use become exhausted of nonusers, the

---

[14] Saffer and Chaloupka, "The Demand for Illicit Drugs."

[15] Morral, McCaffrey, and Paddock, "Reassessing the Marijuana Gateway Effect," and Lynskey et al., "Escalation of Drug Use in Early-Onset Cannabis Users vs. Co-Twin Controls." A conclusion differing from that of Morral et al. is also drawn by Wagner and Anthony, "Into the World of Illegal Drug Use."

number of prospects left to recruit shrinks. Use of the drug begins to ebb, sometimes down to levels prior to the epidemic, sometimes stabilizing at endemic levels. This cycle can take a long time, as heavy-use careers can last many years. Hence, there remains a large number of people who continue to experience the problems of the affliction, even while there are few new cases. The implication is that a small number of epidemic outbreak years could be responsible for a large portion of the drug problem later on.[16]

The use of certain drugs thus comes and, sometimes, goes, control policies notwithstanding. This has important ramifications for interpreting the effectiveness of those policies. If an epidemic is waning for the reasons mentioned above, decreases in use with the passage of time may have little to do with government policies intended to control it. If an epidemic is waxing, control policies may be more effective than they seem if they keep use of the drug from growing faster than it would have without them.

The implication for policymakers framing national drug control goals is as follows: While specific use reduction targets represent laudable objectives, they may be very easy or very difficult to achieve, depending on factors largely outside the government's control. The administration may wind up taking too much credit if the target is met or (worse yet!) not enough, even though it is not met.

U.S. Drug Use Trends in Historical and Global Context

There is good reason for considering the long history of drug use in the United States—and in other countries: It affords some perspective on current U.S. drug problems. If the United States is substantially better off than it has historically been or than other countries are now, perhaps Americans should not expect too much more from drug policy. If there have been times or are now similar societies where drug use is lower, that argues, at the least, for an investigation as to the reasons why.

Fairly good evidence on the history of U.S. drug use goes back as far as the mid-19th century. Since then, use of different drugs has varied considerably. Drug use in general, however, appears to have been quite low in the 1940s and 1950s. For example, in the national drug use surveys, hardly anyone born around 1930 reports having ever used marijuana. Such persons would have reached peak initiation ages during the 1940s and 1950s. For persons born after the early 1950s, and thus reaching drug-using ages in the late 1960s and 1970s, the lifetime prevalence rate is on the order of 50 percent.[17]

What was responsible for the increase in drug use between these generations? Some have placed the blame on cultural forces (or "moral forces"). Antiestablishment attitudes and activities were common among young adults, especially college students, who faced the prospect of being drafted to fight an unpopular war. Drugs became part of the "counter culture" em-

---

[16] On the commonality and rapidity of occurrence of epidemic phenomena, see Winkler, Caulkins, Behrens, and Tragler, "Estimating the Relative Efficiency of Various Forms of Prevention at Different Stages of a Drug Epidemic." David F. Musto advanced the application of the epidemic model to illicit drugs; see, for example, his discussion with respect to the U.S. experience of 1885 to the 1920s in "Lessons of the First Cocaine Epidemic," *The Wall Street Journal,* June 11, 1986, p. 30. For combination of this model with the limiting effects of a finite susceptible population, see, for example, Kleiman, *Against Excess,* pp. 43–44.

[17] For 19th century opium consumption in the United States, see Musto, *The American Disease,* pp. 2–5.

bodying politically and sexually revolutionary perspectives. They were even seen as part of the pathway to a "higher consciousness." While the specific causes and effects can be debated, there was no specific change in government drug policy between the 1950s and 1960s that abetted the efflorescence of the drug culture.[18]

Some current drug problems are common across nations. For example, heroin use at U.S. levels has been found in a number of other wealthy nations (e.g., Australia, Switzerland). And, from 1992 to 1996, youth marijuana use increased in Canada, the Netherlands, Norway, the United Kingdom, *and* the United States. Some European rates for youth have been approaching those experienced in the United States. These common trends are interesting, given differences across those nations in strictures against marijuana use and their enforcement.[19]

Conversely, many developed countries have experienced smaller problems with some other illicit drugs than the United States has. Cocaine in particular has been consumed at lower rates in wealthy European nations, so the higher rates of amphetamine use in some countries still leave them with a total stimulant problem that is smaller than that in the United States.[20]

Such variations are tantalizing. Current U.S. drug policy varies to a modest extent across states, but these differences largely pertain to differences in severity of punishment rather than large-scale alternatives to enforcement. If there is anything to be learned from taking a very different approach, it can only be found elsewhere. Indeed, European experiments with more lax control regimes have been cited by both reformers and defenders of U.S. policy in support of their positions.[21]

The use of the same evidence to arrive at different policy conclusions suggests the strength of prior beliefs and other cultural factors in drug policy formation. Certainly, cultural differences have importantly influenced differences among nations in drug control strategy. Spain, for example, has a long anarchist tradition and a distaste for government control remaining from the years of repression under Franco, so it does not criminalize drug possession. Sweden mandates treatment for drug abuse suspects, even if no arrest has been made, a practice that is consistent with a paternalistic attitude toward abuse of alcohol, a long-standing serious problem there. Sweden also rejects measures that might reduce drug harms but sustain or increase use. In that regard, it is similar to the United States, but the Swedish policy emanates more from a national passion for abstinence than from U.S.-style arguments that harm reduction "sends the wrong message."[22]

---

[18] The characterization of the drug culture in the 1960s is from Bennett, DeIulio, and Walters, *Body Count: Moral Poverty ... And How to Win America's War Against Crime and Drugs,* p. 147, and Musto, *The American Disease,* pp. 247–248.

[19] MacCoun and Reuter, *Drug War Heresies,* p. 124.

[20] In 2002, the lifetime cocaine prevalence rate in the United States was 14.4 percent, and the rate for other stimulants was 9.0 percent. In the part of Germany encompassed by the former Federal Republic, the analogous rates for cocaine and amphetamines were 2.3 percent and 2.3 percent; in France, 1.6 percent and 1.5 percent; in Sweden, 1.0 percent and 2.0 percent; in the United Kingdom, 5.6 percent and 12.3 percent (U.S. rates are from Substance Abuse and Mental Health Services Administration, Office of Applied Studies, "2002 National Survey on Drug Use and Health: Detailed Tables," Table 1.1B, http://oas.samhsa.gov/nhsda/2k2nsduh/Sect1peTabs1to18.pdf. European rates are from the European Monitoring Centre for Drugs and Drug Abuse, *Annual Report 2003: The State of the Drugs Problem in the European Union and Norway,* Statistical Table 1, http://www.emcdda.eu.int/pdfs/stattab01-en/pdf.

[21] On drug policy variation within the United States, see ImpacTeen Illicit Drug Team, *Illicit Drug Policies.* The use of European policies in the U.S. debate is discussed by MacCoun and Reuter, *Drug War Heresies,* pp. 205–206.

[22] MacCoun and Reuter, *Drug War Heresies,* pp. 297–298, 388.

Clearly, drug problems and drug policy vary considerably from one nation to another. If any general global trend can be discerned, it is toward greater availability of drugs. Growing chemical expertise, even in developing countries remote from major markets, and "learning by doing" on the part of producers have multiplied the varieties of drug offered at prices that might attract new consumers or keep old ones interested. At the same time, globalization has affected the illegal drug industry just as it has others. Advances in communication and transportation and the lowering of trade barriers have made it more difficult for national governments to control what passes through their borders, and the growing integration of the global financial system has facilitated money laundering. Producers have shown flexibility in diversifying the drug crops they grow, and refiners in switching their sources between countries, which has made it harder for the United States to isolate its domestic drug market from internationally prevailing lower prices.[23]

[23] On increasing availability and globalization, see Stares, *Global Habit,* pp. 1–9.How Successful Has the War on Drugs Been?

CHAPTER THREE

Why Hasn't the Drug War Been a Greater Success?

To summarize the discussion so far, some simple measures show the war on drugs might be considered successful; others show it generally as a failure. However, such measures do not fully capture all the forces at work and are thus not reliable indicators of success or failure.

Granted the difficulties in arriving at an indisputable assessment, few people seem very satisfied with the accomplishments of U.S. drug policy to date. There appears to be a sense that the United States has spent too many billions of dollars over too many years to have just gone through a decade in which youth drug initiation actually increased and heroin and cocaine dependence declined only modestly. We have shown how the prevailing policy's effectiveness may have been compromised by the dynamics of drug use initiation, intensity, and endurance as they play out over the entire population of drug users and over all drugs. What else may have gone wrong?

Could the Balance among Enforcement, Treatment, and Prevention Have Been Improved?

The war on drugs has been fought through a mix of strategies, notably:

- enforcement, against producers (including those overseas), smugglers, dealers at various levels in U.S. drug markets, and users.
- treatment of heavy users, typically through programs involving many months of counseling
- educational campaigns against drug use, often embodied either in school curricula or in media advertising.

To date, the federal antidrug budget has been tilted toward enforcement. In fiscal year 2003, for example, 53 percent of the president's requested drug control budget was for enforcement, 29 percent for treatment, and 18 percent for prevention. The emphasis on enforcement is often pointed out by critics of prevailing spending priorities. However, that allocation in itself does not imply that enforcement is being overfunded relative to the other approaches. If enforcement were able to produce greater progress toward drug policy goals per dollar spent on it, that might justify the emphasis (although there are considerations other than efficiency). The best available evidence suggests, however, that that is not the case.[1]

In 1997, for example, it was estimated that an additional million dollars spent on federal enforcement activities within U.S. borders five years earlier would have reduced total cocaine consumption by 53 to 98 kilograms (or between 150 and 280 average "careers" of cocaine use). The parallel estimate for treatment of heavy users was 97 to 119 kilograms (between 280 and 340 careers). A case could thus be made that, if the goal has been to reduce drug consumption, at least as much progress toward that goal could have been made within the same total budget by shifting some money from enforcement to treatment. Furthermore, treatment attacks demand directly, whereas enforcement does so by raising prices (insofar as it targets suppliers and not users). Thus, while treatment unambiguously reduces the dollar value of the black market, enforcement may or may not. Whether it does depends on whether the increased prices are more than offset by decreased consumption; the consensus of estimates to date is that they are just offset. Treatment's effects on black market revenue are therefore likely to be greater than enforcement's, so treatment's effects on drug-related crime are also likely to be greater. Such logic does not, however, support the wholesale replacement of enforcement by treatment. The estimates on which the logic is based are valid only at funding levels not far removed from current ones. The effectiveness of treatment may depend on having a big enough enforcement "stick" available as a deterrent. That is, if there were no reason to fear arrest after relapse into usage, fewer treatment participants might make the effort to stay clean.[2]

It should not be very surprising that an enforcement-heavy strategy would have only limited success against the established drug markets now prevailing in the United States. Drug markets are fractionated and local in nature. Drug supply chains are networks, not rigid hierarchies. There is no national organization whose local operations can be crippled through arrests made at the top. Also, arrested sellers are easily replaced.[3]

---

[1] Budget breakdown is calculated from The White House, *National Drug Control Strategy*, 2003, p. 5. An example of a critique of the emphasis on enforcement is that by Drug Policy Alliance, "Outgoing Drug Czar Issues Report Claiming 'Substantial Progress'; Critics Say Drug War Has Failed, New Standards Are Needed," http://www.drugpolicy.org/news/pressroom/pressrelease/pr_january04_01xczar.cfm, quoting Ethan Nadelmann, Lindesmith Center–Drug Policy Foundation.

[2] Cost-effectiveness data are from Caulkins et al., *Mandatory Minimum Drug Sentences*, p. 143. The range limits given are the 25th and 75th percentiles of a Monte Carlo sensitivity analysis; that is, when input parameters were varied randomly, the cost-effectiveness result fell within the range cited 50 percent of the time. The ranges give the impression that treatment's cost-effectiveness might be close to enforcement's, but the probability of that occurring is less than might be expected. That is because if a parameter variation resulted in cost-effectiveness values near the low end of treatment's range, it also tended to result in values in the lower half of enforcement's range. Careers reduced are based on 0.35 kg consumed in the average career, as reported in Caulkins et al., *School-Based Drug Prevention*, p. 21. Treatment's greater effect on drug market revenue and crime is from Caulkins et al., *Mandatory Minimum Drug Sentences*, p. 68, and the limitation to marginal changes is from the same source, p. 79.

[3] On market fractionation and distribution networks, see Jonathan P. Caulkins, "Modeling the Domestic Distribution Network for Illicit Drugs." On seller replacement, see Kleiman, "The Problem of Replacement and the Logic of Drug Law Enforcement."

It might seem odd that treatment could be at least as cost-effective as enforcement at reducing drug sales, when enforcement actually removes drugs and dealers from the street, whereas many treated users go back to using again. Treatment might indeed be less cost-effective if the objective is to get users to quit altogether. But what if the goal is to reduce the quantity of drugs consumed? In that case, just as much is achieved by cutting the use of all individuals by 10 percent as by getting one in ten to quit and leaving the other nine as they were. Fractional individual use reductions can be achieved if the user simply stays clean during treatment, and there is a potential bonus—the treatment client who actually quits permanently. (A study that strongly supports the cost-effectiveness of treatment assumed that, on any given attempt, only 13 percent of those treated quit heavy use, with two-thirds of that 13 percent vulnerable to relapse.)[4]

Treatment is also much cheaper than enforcement in that it costs much less to run a heavy user through treatment than it does to incarcerate a seller (or the user). In addition, since most heavy users consume multiple drugs, driving demand down for one drug by increasing treatment may reduce demand for other drugs as well.[5]

While putting more emphasis on treatment, and perhaps prevention as well, might have led to more success in reducing drug consumption, these alternative approaches can, at best, reduce America's drug problems slowly. They both proceed by small degrees. Treatment succeeds in terms of small percentages of permanent desistance and of small lifetime use reductions by those who do not quit. Likewise, school-based prevention succeeds in terms of small decrements in drug use by program participants (and their social networks) versus nonparticipants. It has been estimated that, based on data from several programs, prevention cuts the average program participant's lifetime marijuana consumption by only 1.7 percent. Prevention's modest success should not be surprising: there is only so much that a program that is often only 30 hours long can do to reverse the effects of thousands of hours of less salutary exposure to television, peers, and so forth. However, prevention is so inexpensive that it is cost-effective and worth pursuing even though its effects are modest.[6]

Both treatment and prevention are also slow to take cumulative effect. Treating a heavy user can bring a stream of benefits lasting many years, but only about one-sixth of those benefits accrue within the year of treatment. The program cost, however, accrues entirely within the first year, so, at the aggregate level, treatment looks less cost-effective than longer sentences

---

[4] It is easy to find much higher average success rates, for example, 20 percent to 69 percent for cocaine use. However, these and most other treatment success data are from large, *uncontrolled, observational* studies instead of controlled experiments. We thus think it prudent to use the results based on the conservative 13 percent figure, from Rydell and Everingham, *Controlling Cocaine,* pp. 19, 24. The 20 to 69 percent is from Duhamel, "Drug Use Outcomes in Four Substance Abuse Treatment Studies."

[5] The costs of treatment and enforcement are from Caulkins et al., *Mandatory Minimum Drug Sentences,* p. 136.

[6] By virtue of lower consumption during treatment alone, a single course of treatment would be expected to cut a heavy user's lifetime cocaine consumption by a quarter of a year's consumption. As noted above, lifetime consumption by a heavy user is almost 18 years at the heavy-use rate. The quarter-year savings is from Rydell and Everingham, *Controlling Cocaine,* p. 24. Prevention's effect on lifetime marijuana consumption is from Caulkins et al., *School-Based Drug Prevention,* p. 158 (conservative delay scenario, medium end-of-program effectiveness, linear decay). The 30-hour program length is for the Life Skills Training Program, as reported by Caulkins et al., *An Ounce of Prevention, a Pound of Uncertainty,* p. 49. Benefits and costs of prevention are compared in Caulkins et al., *School-Based Drug Prevention,* p. 32.

to people with very short time horizons. Colloquially, treatment is like an investment, arresting and incarcerating sellers for a year or two is like paying as you go, and extending sentences from 1–2 years to 5–10 years is like buying with a credit card. (See Figure 3.1, in which the cost-effectiveness of different control strategies are compared across horizons of 1 to 15 years, that is, no benefits or costs beyond the horizon are counted.) Likewise, prevention can do nothing about the large number of adults who have been using for a long time; it can only reduce the rate of recruitment into the pool of users. When it comes to immediacy and certainty of effect, enforcement thus has the advantage. If a drug dealer sets up business across the street, bringing enforcement to bear will get the problem addressed. Increasing the number of treatment slots will not.[7]

It is important to pay attention to the dates for which cost-effectiveness estimates apply because, as we have discussed, drug use is not static. Rates of initiation and heavy use change over the course of epidemics such as that for cocaine. Treatment of heavy users could not much affect total consumption early in an epidemic, before there are many heavy users. Neither can much be expected of prevention programs run late in an epidemic, when initiation has dropped off. (Such programs may help prevent the next epidemic, however.) Like prevention, enforcement may be most cost-effective at reducing drug use if employed early. Later, when the market has matured and supplies and dealers are plentiful, it is more difficult for enforcement to limit production and distribution than it is to do so earlier, when the targets are fewer. On

Figure 3.1
Longer Sentences Look Better When the Evaluation Horizon Is Very Short

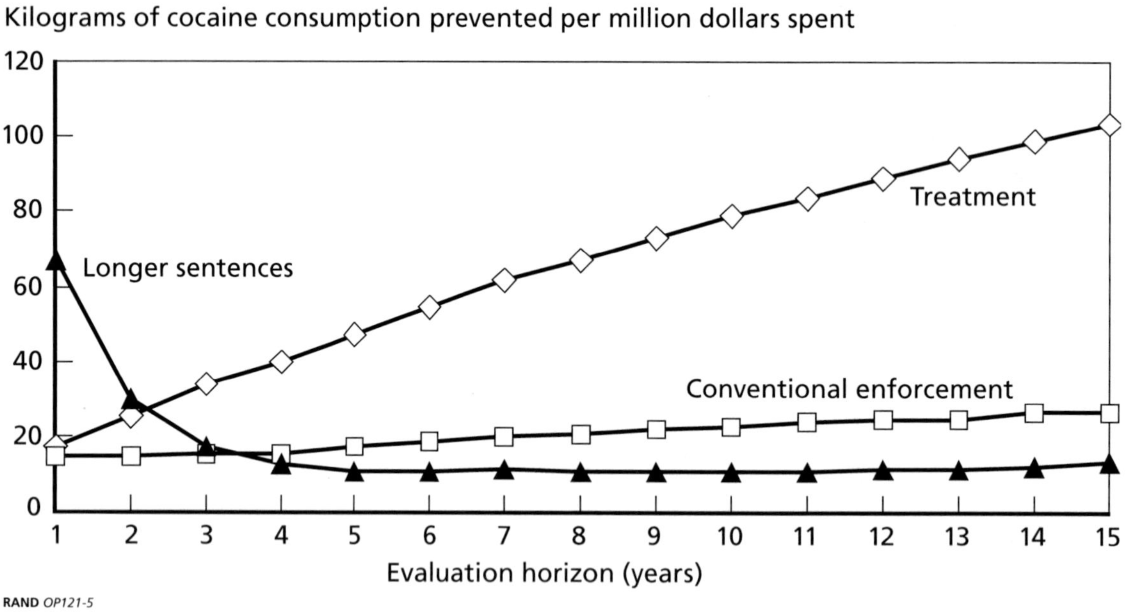

SOURCE: From Caulkins et al., *Mandatory Minimum Drug Sentences*, p. 36.

[7] Distribution of costs and benefits of treatment over time is from Caulkins et al., *Mandatory Minimum Drug Sentences,* pp. 100, 102.

the other hand, enforcement actions can be relevant and valuable throughout an epidemic if their purpose is not simply to reduce use but also the harmful consequences of drug use. For example, one would always like to see some level of enforcement directed to reducing the involvement of juveniles in the drug trade, by targeting dealers who employ them.[8]

Although the effectiveness of drug policies varies over the course of an epidemic, they are largely crafted and implemented as if drug use were indeed static. Treatment's share of the annual federal antidrug budget, for example, stayed between 17 and 20 percent from 1987 to 1995, as the nature of the drug problem changed considerably. There is little evidence to suggest that the mix of drug control strategies varies substantially in response to the evolving threat—or to suggest that the value of that kind of responsiveness is even recognized.[9]

Could the Balance among Enforcement Strategies Have Been Improved?

Enforcement is itself a varied collection of activities, and it is directed at different stages in the drug production "pipeline":[10]

- Source country control: financial, technical, intelligence, and equipment aid to source countries attempting to eradicate drug crops, shut down processing facilities, reduce exports, and bring to justice those involved in the drug trade.
- Interdiction en route to the United States: actions by the Coast Guard and by agents of the Bureau of Immigration and Customs Enforcement to interrupt the movement of drugs between the source country and U.S. borders.
- Domestic enforcement: seizure of drugs and other assets within U.S. borders and the arrest, prosecution, and punishment of drug dealers and users.

At each stage it is important to distinguish three types of effects. First, enforcement can create temporary disruption by "surprising" the supply network with unexpected new tactics or intensities of effort. That creates shortages and price spikes. As already suggested, surprise disruption is very hard to achieve within the United States for a mature, mass-market drug. Successes include, in the early 1970s, the disruption of the "French connection" for heroin through arrests, Turkey's ban on poppy growing, and the spraying of the Mexican marijuana crop, and, in 1989, Colombia's attack on the Medellin cocaine cartel. Such successes have predominantly been in the source zone or sometimes in transit, where a smaller number of

---

[8] The discussion of policies responsive to epidemic stages is based on Behrens et al., "Optimal Control of Drug Epidemics," and Tragler, Caulkins, and Feichtinger, "Optimal Dynamic Allocation of Treatment and Enforcement in Illicit Drug Control." On focused law enforcement, see Caulkins, "Law Enforcement's Role in a Harm Reduction Regime."

[9] Treatment's share is from The White House, *The National Drug Control Strategy, 1996,* pp. 318–319. ONDCP's estimates of treatment's share are probably liberal. (See Murphy et al., *Improving Anti-Drug Budgeting,* pp. 104–107.) However, there is no reason to believe that the consistency from year to year is an artifact.

[10] We here follow the paradigm used in Rydell and Everingham, *Controlling Cocaine,* p. xii.

organizations is responsible for a larger share of the market. Unfortunately, even at those production stages, notable successes are infrequent.[11]

Second, enforcement can affect the severity of drug-related consequences for each kilogram consumed, even if it does not affect the quantity consumed. Selective enforcement against dealers who are particularly violent, corrupting, or otherwise noxious might reduce drug-related consequences if any replacement of those dealers is with less noxious ones. Unfortunately, there is, as of yet, little to no quantitative evidence concerning this second class of effects at any of the three major production pipeline stages.

Third, enforcement can "tax" the supply chain by imposing costs and complications that—at the aggregate level—are anticipated and adjusted for. That is not to say that any individual anticipates arrest or any organization expects elimination. However, if, as has been the case for some years, the United States annually seizes 100 metric tons of cocaine and consumes 300 metric tons, the supply chain will plan to ship about 400 tons next year. Such market responsiveness does not mean that anticipated seizures are ineffective. The 300 tons still has to be sold at higher prices to compensate for the 100 tons that are seized.[12]

This type of effect has been well studied in the case of cocaine in the early 1990s. Analyses suggest that domestic enforcement was one-third again as cost-effective as interdiction and three times as cost-effective as source country control at reducing cocaine consumption (see Figure 3.2). That is, assume that an extra million dollars were spent arresting, prosecuting, and incarcerating typical dealers under the sentencing regimen prevailing before the introduction of mandatory minimums. Cocaine consumption would then decrease by an amount three times what it would if the extra million dollars were spent on source country control. The reasons are not difficult to understand. Production costs in the Andean countries are small, and the amounts of product required are not large by agricultural standards. There is plenty of land available to grow the coca needed to produce the 400 tons of cocaine shipped each year to the United States. Even if local production costs were to go up substantially, the rise might still be small compared to the huge mark-up between the source country and the street, so the price users pay might not be much affected.[13]

Interdiction is not much less problematic in this regard than source country control. Four hundred tons may sound like a lot, but it is a negligible fraction of the legitimate commerce

---

[11] On enforcement surprises and their effects, see Caulkins, "Measurement and Analysis of Drug Problems and Drug Control Efforts." On successes (and qualifications thereto), see Kleiman, *Against Excess,* pp. 132–133. On the limits to enforcement more generally, see Reuter, "The Limits of Supply-Side Drug Control."

[12] From 1992 through 2000, federal cocaine seizures ranged from 101 to 132 metric tons, according to The White House, *National Drug Control Strategy,* 2003, "Data Supplement," p. 55. For the same period, U.S. cocaine consumption ranged from 259 to 346 metric tons, according to Abt Associates, *What America's Users Spend on Illegal Drugs,* p. 19.

[13] On the investment required to grow coca: In 1990, it cost $700 per hectare (2.47 acres) to grow coca in the Upper Huallaga Valley of Peru, an amount that would generate $1,680 in profit to the farmer. It has been estimated that coca is grown on less than 1 percent of the land on which it could be cultivated in Bolivia and Peru alone. It takes $700 worth of coca leaf to produce cocaine valued at $150,000 on the street (Riley, *Snow Job?* pp. 126, 142, 83). Thus, doubling the price of the leaf would add only $700 or about 0.5 percent to the street price. Indeed, sharp fluctuations in coca leaf prices over the last decade have not been reflected in retail cocaine prices in the United States. (See Reuter, "The Limits of Supply-Side Drug Control.") It has, however, been argued that the pricing structure of the cocaine market is multiplicative, that is, that an x percent increase in costs at the source results in an x percent increase in costs on the street. In that case, source country control (and interdiction) could yield appreciable street price increases. See Crane, Rivolo, and Comfort, *An Experimental Examination of Counterdrug Interdiction Program Effectiveness,* pp. II-1 and II-2.

Figure 3.2
Cost-Effectiveness Comparison of Enforcement Strategies

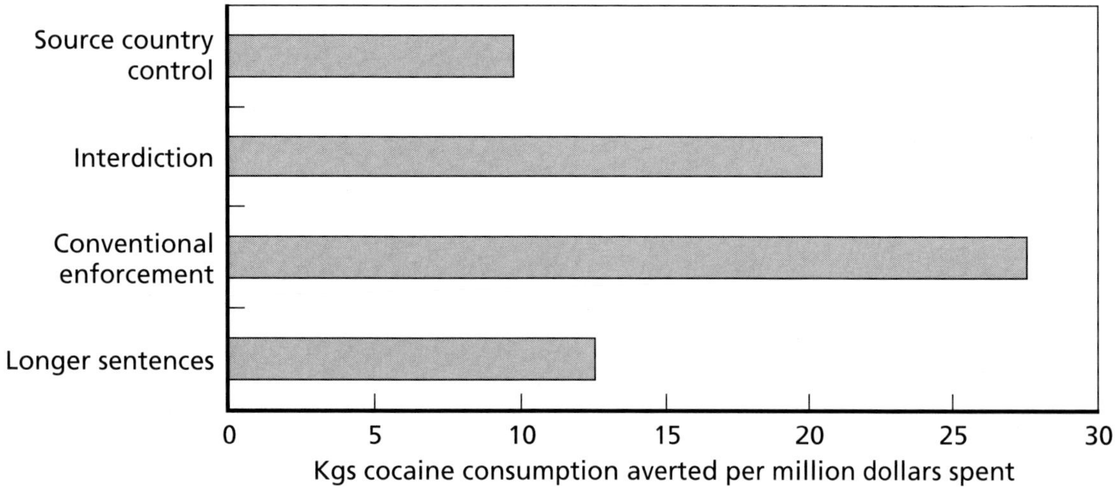

RAND *OP121-5a*

SOURCE: Caulkins et al., *Mandatory Minimum Drug Sentences,* pp. 45, 143.

across U.S. borders every year. Colombia, for example, ships an average of 170,000 tons of coffee to the United States each year. Because the drugs are worth many times their weight in gold, the financial rewards justify using quite sophisticated means of camouflaging the contraband. Attempts to shut down prevailing supply routes and means can be circumvented at modest cost by use of alternate routes and means.[14]

Domestic enforcement collectively may look good by comparison, but not all elements of domestic enforcement are equally cost-effective. Figure 3.2 shows the cost-effectiveness of a fourth alternative: using the extra million dollars to extend to mandatory-minimum lengths the sentences of typical arrested dealers. This incarceration-only alternative would be less than half as cost-effective as expanding the full suite of conventional enforcement measures under a regime of shorter sentences. Incarceration is problematic because, while it does place high costs on drug dealers, it is also costly to the public. Furthermore, which drug dealers incur incarceration risk? With mandatory minimum sentences, it is often those physically in possession of a given quantity of drugs, and those are rarely the dealers near the head of the supply chain. In contrast, not only do drugs and other property seized at the time of arrest represent a significant cost to dealers, but accomplishing those seizures has a lower public cost than incarceration.[15]

---

[14] The coffee import number is the average over 1997–2001 data from U.S. Department of Agriculture, Commodity and Marketing Programs, "U.S. General Imports of Agricultural, Fish, and Forestry Products from Colombia."

[15] In 1992, Kleiman, *Against Excess,* p. 140, estimated that a year in prison costs a cocaine dealer $25,000 to $50,000. The taxpayer cost of a year in prison at that time was approximately $25,000, according to Caulkins et al., *Mandatory Minimum Drug Sentences,* p. 86. The type of drug dealers incurring incarceration risk is from Caulkins et al., *Mandatory Minimum Drug Sentences,* pp. 15–16, 18. It costs about $22,000 to arrest and adjudicate a cocaine suspect, while in federal cases assets forfeited amount on average to perhaps $64,000, of which $15,000 are nondrug assets that can offset the arrest costs (averages account for zeroes in the case of not-guilty dispositions; from Caulkins et al., *Mandatory Minimum Drug Sentences,* pp. 121, 123).

In sum, then, the drug war might have achieved more if

- policy had been more sensitive to the particular strengths and weaknesses of enforcement, treatment, and prevention and had been more responsive to the changing nature of drug use
- more of the funding expansion since the late 1980s had been allocated to treatment rather than enforcement
- less emphasis had been placed on giving very long sentences, particularly when those sentences were mostly triggered by the quantity possessed at the time of arrest.

Thus, if the goal had been to reduce total consumption by some amount, that could have been done more cheaply by treating heavy users than by incarcerating dealers for longer periods. From that perspective, choosing the incarceration option has thus wasted money that could have been spent on other aspects of enforcement (e.g., against other crimes) or on achieving other social purposes. The official national goal, however, has been decreasing the fraction of the population that uses, and, as suggested above, treatment's cost-effectiveness at achieving that goal may be lower.

More generally, we should emphasize here that we are not attempting to assign blame. Information on costs and effectiveness of the various strategies was unavailable as federal spending on drug control was rising rapidly in the late 1980s and early 1990s. It is unfortunate, however, that little was invested in efforts to evaluate the strategies on which large amounts were being expended. That was particularly true of the various enforcement approaches; much more has been invested in evaluating prevention and treatment, on which less is spent.[16]

[16] For data on the rise in the federal drug control budget (which quadrupled between 1986 and 1992), see The White House, *The National Drug Control Strategy, 1996: Program, Resources, and Evaluation.* On the lack of research on enforcement relative to the money spent on it, see Reuter, "Why Can't We Make Prohibition Work Better?" Why Hasn't the Drug War Been a Greater Success?

CHAPTER FOUR

What About Bonuses and Collateral Damage?

To this point, we have been discussing whether the drug war has been successful and how it might have been more so in terms of its central goals of reducing drug use and use-related harms. Drug control policy cannot, however, be evaluated solely on the basis of whether it has achieved its stated aims. It has had side effects, both good and bad.

Though it has not always been a formally stated aim, reduction of the crime associated with drug use and sales would be regarded by many people as an important (and expected) "bonus." Drug control may indeed have been partly responsible for the decline in crime rates in general that the nation experienced during the 1990s. If the additional resources devoted to enforcement have decreased consumption, as the cost-effectiveness studies suggest, then crime by persons under the influence should have gone down. Moreover, greater emphasis on incarceration may have kept persons off the street who may otherwise have committed crimes other than drug offenses, either because of their expensive drug habits or because of their other characteristics.[1]

On the negative side, it has been argued that the drug war has imposed "collateral damage" in several realms, for example,[2]

- erosion of civil liberties
- erosion of police integrity
- exacerbation of drug-related harms such as the spread of HIV infection
- generation of consequences beyond the criminal justice system; such sanctions have negative effects on families and communities.

---

[1] The violent crime rate has fallen from 758 per 100,000 persons in 1991 to 504 in 2001 (Federal Bureau of Investigation, *Crime in the United States, 2001,* p. 64).

[2] For erosion of civil liberties and police integrity, see Bertram et al., *Drug War Politics,* pp. 46–50. Sources for the other two items follow.

The first of these is an important matter of justice and values but is not one to whose assessment we can contribute analytically. The second has not been measured in any systematic way. We offer some brief observations on the other two, both of which have implications for the equity of the distribution of drug control costs across racial, ethnic, and economic groups.

Endemic use of heroin and other injection drugs has promoted infection with HIV, hepatitis C virus (HCV), and other infectious diseases. The root cause of this infection is thus not federal drug policy, but that policy has exacerbated the problem by seeking primarily to reduce use instead of use-related harm. For example, needle exchanges might reduce HIV and HCV infection. However, funding of such programs is explicitly banned at the federal level on the theory that they promote drug abuse (a theory unsupported by research). The current rate at which HIV and HCV are spreading may thus be viewed as a side effect of the campaign against drugs, to the extent that it is higher than it would have been otherwise.[3]

By the drug war's "consequences beyond the criminal justice system," we mean its effects on families and communities and effects on the offender beyond fines, forfeitures, and incarceration. These effects have been concentrated in racial and ethnic minority communities, because most of them are triggered by conviction of a drug offense, and drug offenders are disproportionately minority. (In 1996, blacks alone constituted 53 percent of drug convicts at the state level, where the great majority of drug cases are prosecuted.) Among the consequences are the following:[4]

- Family disruption. Black children are nine times more likely to have a parent in prison than are white children.[5]
- Limitations in access to family support payments. Conviction of any drug offense permanently bars the individual from receiving food stamps or Temporary Aid for Needy Families. (However, the weak available evidence suggests that there is little enforcement of this by state welfare agencies; they tend not to keep track of criminal histories.)
- Eviction from public housing. Drug abuse and convictions are used by public housing authorities to deny access and to evict tenants, including the families of offenders, not just the offenders themselves.
- Limitations in access to student aid. Those convicted of drug possession are ineligible for federal student aid for at least a year.
- Deportation of immigrants. Drug felonies are responsible for 41 percent of deportations executed on the basis of criminal convictions. Such deportations disproportionately affect minority communities; the significance of this effect is uncertain.

---

[3] Predominance of injection drug use in the spread of HIV and HCV infection is from the National Institute on Drug Abuse, "NIDA InfoFacts: Drug Abuse and AIDS," http://www.nida.nih.gov/Infofax/DrugAbuse.html, and "NIDA Community Drug Alert Bulletin—Hepatitis," May 2000, http://www.drugabuse.gov/HepatitisAlert/HepatitisAlert.html, both as posted June 11, 2003. On the evolution of needle exchange funding policy and the relations among needle exchange, HIV propagation, and drug abuse, see Vlahov et al., "Needle Exchange Programs for the Prevention of Human Immunodeficiency Virus Infection."

[4] Percentage of black convicts and predominance of state-level prosecutions are from Maguire and Pastore, *Sourcebook of Criminal Justice Statistics 2000.* Sanctions are from Iguchi et al., "Elements of Well-Being Affected by Criminalizing the Drug User."

[5] Mumola, *Incarcerated Parents and Their Children,* p. 2.

- Employment restrictions. Felony convicts are disqualified from serving in the military or holding a government job.
- Reduction in political power. In most states, paroled felons cannot vote. In 1998, it was estimated that 13 percent of all black men had been temporarily or permanently disenfranchised and that that figure would continue to grow if prevailing enforcement levels were maintained.[6]

Most of these effects arise from extending sanctions to other domains of public life once the criminal justice system sanctions have lapsed. Because they remove social supports from reentering convicts, they may increase recidivism. They do, however, have the benefit of keeping the protected institutions free of those who have abused the public trust and who may be more likely than the average person to use drugs in the future. They also may add to the effect of criminal sanctions in deterring those who would use drugs, and they add to the atmosphere of public disapprobation of drug use that may have some more general deterrent effect.

Enforcement strategy has other implications for equity. For various reasons, the war on drugs appears to be fought mainly in minority communities. Minorities, for example, are much more likely to be imprisoned for violating drug laws than are whites. Criticisms that U.S. drug policy reflects prevailing racial and class privileges have been well aired elsewhere. It can be argued, however, that enforcement is appropriately focused on sellers, who locate disproportionately in minority communities. Whether enforcement is the right strategy to direct toward users is controversial, but if so, it is relevant that frequent cocaine use is much more common in urban poverty areas, which tend also to be minority communities, than elsewhere. While exposure to the high costs of conviction and associated sanctions is principally borne by poorer, minority communities, the relatively modest household costs of funding the campaign against drugs are borne mainly by households with income above the median.[7]

Such racial disparities feed racial tensions. Minorities see that most drug convicts are black or brown and feel they are being unfairly targeted. White suburbanites may see the same disparity as evidence that drug epidemics emanate from inner-city neighborhoods to engulf innocent suburban schoolchildren. While racial dissension has not yet become the central issue in the debate over drug policy, it complicates the search for a solution: Inner-city communities are often skeptical about enforcement, while suburban communities may feel that at root, it's not their problem.[8]

---

[6] Fellner, Mauer, and Hirschfield, "Losing the Vote: the Impact of Felony Disenfranchisement Laws in the United States," Chapters III (Table 2) and IV.

[7] In 2001, 58 percent of prisoners in state prison on drug charges were black (calculated from prisoner counts in Harrison and Beck, *Prisoners in 2001,* p. 13). On the racial profile of the drug war, see Bertram et al., *Drug War Politics,* pp. 36–45. On the concentration of drug sales in minority communities, see Kleiman, *Against Excess,* pp. 111–112, and Tonry, *Malign Neglect.* Frequency of cocaine use in poverty areas is from Brownsberger, "Prevalence of Frequent Cocaine Use in Urban Poverty Areas." Individual income tax receipts account for about half of all federal revenue, and in 2000, 96 percent of all individual income tax receipts were from the top half of the income distribution (Internal Revenue Service, "Tax Stats at a Glance," http://www.irs.gov/taxstats/article/0,,id=102886,00.html, as posted June 17, 2003, and Hoffman, *Who Pays the Federal Individual Income Tax?* p. 1).

[8] On minority and white views regarding the drug war and the drug problem, see Bertram et al., *Drug War Politics,* pp. 42–45, and Courtwright, *Forces of Habit,* p. 202.What about Bonuses and Collateral Damage?

CHAPTER FIVE

Why No Course Corrections?

According to the evidence we have reviewed here, the war on drugs has not well met its own objectives and may have had some important negative side effects. The perceptions of the general public have not been more favorable over the years. In 1995, 72 percent of adults declared that the war on drugs had had no effect on drug use in their community. In 1999, 72 percent of registered voters had the (mistaken) impression that drug use had increased (41 percent said "greatly") over the previous ten years. And half of those asked agreed with the statement, "We are unable to win the war on drugs regardless of what the President and Congress do." Similarly, in March 2001, 74 percent of adult Americans thought the United States was losing the drug war.[1]

Yet U.S. policymakers, with at least the tacit support of their skeptical electorate, have retained the long-standing enforcement-oriented policy. Why has the same strategy been pursued despite widespread perceptions that it has not succeeded? Why haven't promising alternative strategies, even within the broad parameters of prohibition, been tried?

Various reasons have been advanced: that enforcement proponents have narrowed the debate, partly by ignoring or maligning critics; that dissenting politicians cannot win by being less tough on drugs than their opponents; that drug use is seen as a moral failing deserving of punishment, not a health problem deserving of treatment. Voters and politicians may perceive that incarceration has more reliably predictable effects than prevention or treatment. They may not be interested in individual use reductions and other half-measures; they may want to see their children free of addiction risk and addicts cured by treatment. It's natural to want to place

---

[1] Percentage of adults declaring that the war on drugs had had no effect is from the LexisNexis Web site, Roper Center at the University of Connecticut, "Public Opinion Online," citing *U.S. News and World Report,* May 1993, citing Texas A&M Public Policy Institute, *Crime in America,* July 1995; 1999 data are from the LexisNexis Web site, Roper Center, "Public Opinion Online," citing Family Research Council, "Annual Survey on Drug Policy," 1999; both as posted April 19, 2002; 2001 response is from Pew Research Center for the People & the Press, "Interdiction and Incarceration Are Still Top Remedies," March 21, 2001, http://people-press.org/reports/display.php3?ReportID=16.

the blame on someone else, so interdiction and source country control are popular measures because they assign responsibility for the drug problem to foreigners and also are relatively inexpensive. As we have pointed out, few voters feel drug policy's negative consequences in their communities. State legislators may find it easier, less of an immediate burden on the budget, and more sympathetic with public outrage to lengthen sentences than to empower more nuanced adjudication efforts or augment treatment funding.[2]

This last approach may seem to contradict what we said earlier: incarceration is expensive, not cheap. However, states generally do not require that sentencing enhancements be accompanied by funding actions. Prisons are already constructed and staffed, so filling them up looks cost-free. Thus, there is no specific tax consequence to offset the political value of lengthening sentences. Furthermore, a *county's* district attorney deciding to more zealously pursue incarceration can take free advantage of the *state*-provided prison resource. Eventually, however, the bill comes due, and some states have begun to take a harder look at their sentencing policies; the federal government, however, is still pushing for the longest prison terms possible.[3]

We also must concede that it is easier to criticize than to propose sound alternatives, that the evidence in favor of alternative approaches, while suggestive, is not strong enough to persuade skeptics. And some argue in favor of the opposite proposition, that the current approach is successful, or rather, that more of the same could be even more successful. However, as pointed out above, evidence for or against the effectiveness of specific enforcement strategies is scarce. This reflects a tradition of scanty reliance on research and analysis within the criminal justice system as a whole.[4]

Finally, below the President, there is no one person responsible for U.S. drug policy. The drug "czar" is not a czar. He has no direct authority over the drug programs in federal agencies other than his own, and the latter accounts for only a small fraction of the drug control budget. He has no authority whatsoever over drug control at state and local levels. Drug policy formation is fragmented across many agencies at all levels of government. Broad, crosscutting, nationwide shifts in policy could thus be difficult to effect. The impetus must emanate from legislative bodies, and, as we have noted, elected officials are not often interested in promoting a more nuanced drug policy.[5]

There are thus many possible reasons for drug policy inertia. Whatever the real reasons might be, they must be acknowledged and addressed as part of any strategy to move U.S. drug policy in more productive directions.

---

[2] Reuter, "Why Does Research Have So Little Impact on American Drug Policy?", and Bertram et al., *Drug War Politics,* p. 151.

[3] On prison space as an apparently free common resource, see Benson and Rasmussen, "The Context of Drug Policy." On reservations at the state level but not the federal, see Sullivan, "Missouri Sentencing Changes Stem Need for Prison Growth," and Zielbauer, "Rethinking the Key Thrown Away."

[4] On the need for more enforcement, see Bennett, DeIulio, and Walters, *Body Count,* pp. 187–190, where, of five "priorities for effective action," four are enforcement-related. On the dearth of evidence for its effectiveness, see Reuter, "Why Does Research Have So Little Impact on American Drug Policy?" Regarding the lack of research on the criminal justice system more generally, see Blumstein and Petersilia, "Investing in Criminal Justice Research," and Wilson, "What, if Anything, Can the Federal Government Do to Reduce Crime?"

[5] On the limited power of the ONDCP, see Musto, *The American Disease,* pp. 280–281, and Bertram et al., *Drug War Politics,* p. 132. On policy fragmentation, see Haaga and Reuter, "The Limits of the Czar's Ukase."

CHAPTER SIX

How Might U.S. Drug Problems and Policies Evolve?

Another prerequisite to any vision of future drug policy is an understanding of the future evolution of drug use and other drug-related problems. It would also help to consider how drug policy might evolve in response to such trends, and thus whether reforms, if they are advisable, might be either easier or more difficult to accomplish in the future.

Of course, there might be less need to think about the future if the past suggested little likelihood of change. And so it has been with the recent past. America's drug problem, at least as far as the big three (cocaine, heroin, and marijuana) are concerned, has settled, superficially at least, into a time of stability or, at most, predictable change: Overall usage has been steady or down some, and while initiation has rebounded, there has been nothing as dramatic as the propagation of the crack epidemic in the 1980s. As discussed above, this stability in drug problems is mirrored by an even longer-standing stability in drug policy, centered on enforcement and punishment.[1]

The inertia of the past decade or more is an exception, however. The 1960s, 1970s, and 1980s were periods of dramatic change in drug use: the spread of marijuana, the heroin epidemic, the explosion in cocaine initiation, and the spread of crack and street markets. And in thinking about the future, we should not limit ourselves to the recent history of the United States. Policy was quite different a century ago in America, and in recent years it has changed rapidly in other developed countries.[2]

---

[1] The number of crack initiates more than tripled between 1975 and 1979, from 30,000 to 107,000, then more than tripled again, to 370,000, by 1989 (Substance Abuse and Mental Health Services Administration, *Results from the 2001 National Household Survey on Drug Abuse: Volume III. Detailed Tables,* Table 4.3A, citing the 1999, 2000, and 2001 NHSDAs).

[2] On the spread of marijuana and heroin use in the 1960s, see Musto, *The American Disease,* pp. 247–248. The number of annual cocaine initiates topped out in 1983 at 1.48 million, having more than doubled since 1974, when there were 582,000 (Substance Abuse and Mental Health Services Administration, *Results from the 2001 National Household Survey on Drug Abuse: Volume III. Detailed Tables,* Table 4.2A, citing the 1999, 2000, and 2001 NHSDAs).

While we have so far in this paper drawn from published research and expert judgment, there is no guide to the future. If anything, stability in problems and in policy has fostered inattention to the future. This inattention is reinforced by the lack of vested interests in the future of drug policy and problems. Politicians have short time horizons, and researchers write only about what their methods can address, so they say little about the policy future. Importantly, in the illicit-drug arena there is no legitimate industry to support the bevy of consultants who generate alternative futures in many other policy domains, for example, defense and energy.

In the absence of a published literature, we convened a panel of 14 drug experts from across the nation for a colloquium in August 2002. It was the panel's consensus that there were many reasons to think drug problems and policy could change rapidly again over the next 5 to 20 years. In summarizing some of those reasons here, we divide them into three categories:

- "Drivers" or factors influencing drug problems and policy, which could grow stronger or weaker.
- Assumptions about the future context that could fail.
- "Wild cards," or unexpected developments that could change the course of problems and policy.

Note that in the following we are not attempting to forecast any one specific drug problem or policy future as the most likely. We show, instead, that there is a range of possibilities that may represent departures from current trends.

What Drivers Could Change in Strength?

Many factors could grow stronger or weaker in the coming years and drive problems and policy off their current course. Colloquium participants focused here on factors outside drug use that shape key aspects of it, factors whose future course seems reasonably predictable but whose effects on drug use are less obvious.

- Recent decades have seen a shift from communitarian, religiously based moral codes of conduct to individualist, secular values. This shift has influenced almost every aspect of the government's role as moral arbiter; these include rules about sexual behavior, abortion, and gambling. As suggested above, the shift has not extended so dramatically to drug control. Drug policy and problems will be strongly affected by how long the drug exception holds out. Conversely, a general return to communitarian values could more firmly lock strict drug prohibition in against the effects of any liberalizing trends.[3]
- Trends in the use of licit substances may affect the use of illicit drugs. For example, tobacco use has been decreasing. Cigarette smokers are more likely to use marijuana than

[3] The shift from communitarian to individualist values is from Courtwright, "Which Sides Are You On?"

nonsmokers. If that relationship is not just coincidental, and if tobacco use keeps falling, marijuana use could also fall.[4]

- Some states have shown a willingness to experiment with drug policy; for example, California and eight other states have allowed the cultivation of marijuana at home for medicinal purposes. This experimentation creates tension with the federal government. Cases pitting federal control against state prerogatives are beginning to come before the courts, and the decisions may affect drug policy.[5]
- The war on terrorism could influence drug use and policy. Any terrorist attacks linked to the drug trade might increase the stigmatization associated with drug use. Also, greater attention to border control could increase the quantity of drugs seized, but large reassignments of interdiction resources to counterterrorist duties may take a toll on enforcement pressure against traffickers. The evidence is mixed as to which of these effects has predominated to date.[6]
- The globalization of trade has contributed to the availability of drugs and complicated their control. Lower customs barriers mean easier smuggling, and drugs are no exception to globalization's worldwide diversification of markets; more drugs are more globally available than was the case 20 years ago, and that trend can be expected to continue.[7]
- Violent crime has been associated with drug use, both in the minds of the public and in reality. The reduction of violent crime since the early 1990s has made it easier to talk about alternatives to the criminal justice approach to drug policy. If the violent-crime rate rebounds at the same time that "softer" approaches to drug policy are being implemented, there could be a backlash against such approaches.[8]

---

[4] The percentage of the U.S. population currently smoking was 33.3 percent in 1979, 25.3 percent in 1990, and 23.1 percent in 2000 (National Center for Health Statistics [NCHS], *Health, United States, 2002,* p. 196, citing NCHS, National Health Interview Survey). In 2001, 14.9 percent of tobacco smokers reported using marijuana or hashish in the preceding 30 days, whereas only 2.2 percent of nonsmokers reported doing so (Substance Abuse and Mental Health Services Administration, *Results from the 2001 National Household Survey on Drug Abuse: Volume III. Detailed Tables,* Table 6.7B).

[5] On medical-marijuana laws and tensions between the states and the federal government, see Pacula et al., "State Medical Marijuana Laws," pp. 413–439, and Ehisen, "States Keep Medical Marijuana Debate Alive." Besides California, the eight states approving medical-marijuana laws permitting home cultivation are Alaska, Washington, Oregon, Nevada, Colorado, and Maine (all by ballot measure) and Hawaii and Vermont (by the legislature). Vermont's law was to take effect on July 1, 2004 (Allen, "State Will Legalize Medical Marijuana Use"). The U.S. Supreme Court has recently heard a case stemming from California's medical marijuana law (see Greenhouse, "States Rights Defense Falters in Medical Marijuana Case").

[6] The amount of cocaine seized by Customs and Border Protection (formerly the Customs Service) fell 12.1 percent from fiscal year 2001 to 2002, and the amount of marijuana seized fell 8.6 percent; however, the amount of heroin seized rose by 14.0 percent (*U.S. Customs Service—America's Frontline: Performance and Annual Report Fiscal Year 2002,* p. 35).

[7] See Stares, *Global Habit,* pp. 1, 27–46, 55–56.

[8] When asked to rate the importance of various factors as causes of crime, 59 percent rated drug use "critical" in 2000 and 64 percent did so in 1993—in both cases more than the percentage assigning a "critical" rating to any of eight other potential causes, for example, television violence, the decline of religion, poor school quality (Maguire and Pastore, eds., *Sourcebook of Criminal Justice Statistics 2000,* p. 130, citing The Gallup Organization, Inc., *The Gallup Poll).* It has been estimated that 32 percent of homicides, 10 percent of sexual assaults, 40 percent of aggravated assaults, and 30 percent of robberies are drug-related (Caulkins et al., *Mandatory Minimum Drug Sentences,* p. 183). As one metric of the ease of talking about alternatives, in 1998, 28 percent of Americans thought that marijuana should be legalized, up from 16 percent in 1990 (Maguire and Pastore, *Sourcebook of Criminal Justice Statistics 1999,* pp. 150–151, citing National Opinion Research Center, General Social Surveys).

What Widely Maintained Assumptions Might Fail?

Drug problems and policy can track a familiar course in the future only if certain assumptions supporting the current trends are maintained. Some of those assumptions seem safe, such as a belief that the volume of legitimate cross-border trade will continue to be very large relative to drug smuggling, making it difficult to "seal the borders." Colloquium participants believed that other assumptions (phrased as questions below) that have been valid in the past are more vulnerable to reversal, or at least more vulnerable than is commonly assumed.

- Will the current "big three" illicit drugs continue to dominate drug problems? Cocaine, heroin, and marijuana together account for most illicit drug use in the United States and most of the associated crime. The price of ecstasy, however, is likely to drop, triggering expanded use. Likewise, if methamphetamine use in the eastern United States caught up to levels in the West, national methamphetamine-related crime and market revenues could surpass those of heroin. Either of these occurrences could stress the enforcement and treatment systems.[9]
- Will policy continue to treat different illegal drugs much the same? This is an important issue because drugs vary greatly in the burdens they place on society. The most obvious candidate for differential treatment is marijuana. While laws against using and selling marijuana are strict in most jurisdictions, enforcement has been more lax than that for other drugs. If that distinction were to be codified, would marijuana be uniquely distinguished from the common, expensive, "hard" drugs, or would exceptions be made for other substances too?[10]
- Will expanded investment in drug treatment continue to be unpopular? As Alan I. Leshner, then director of the National Institute on Drug Abuse, wrote in 1999, "[T]here are now extensive data showing that addiction is eminently treatable if the treatment is well-delivered and tailored to the needs of the particular patient." However, that drug dependence can be treated in ways that benefit the patient and, indirectly, the public at large, does not mean that treatment can cure the dependence the way antibiotics can cure an infection. Through some combination of unrealistic expectations, underappreciation of actual performance, and qualms about publicly funded programs whose direct benefi-

[9] In results from the Arrestee Drug Abuse Monitoring system, all 12 sites in which at least 10 percent of arrestees tested positive for methamphetamine use were west of the Mississippi River; seven of the eight sites in which no arrestees tested positive for methamphetamines were east of the Mississippi (National Institute of Justice, *2000 Arrestee Drug Abuse Monitoring: Annual Report,* p. 8).

[10] It has been estimated (Caulkins et al., *School-Based Drug Prevention,* p. 104), that 59 percent of the social costs of illicit-drug use are due to cocaine, 25 percent to heroin or other opiates, 9 percent to marijuana or hashish, and 7 percent to all other drugs. As MacCoun and Reuter argue in *Drug War Heresies* (p. 341), "For purposes of the legalization debate, marijuana is the cutting edge drug, the only politically plausible candidate for major legal change, at least depenalization and perhaps even outright legalization. Compared to other drugs, the harms, physiological or behavioral, are less severe, and the drug is better integrated into the culture. It has been used by a large share of the population at some time in their lives." Thirty-six states currently classify marijuana as the federal government does, that is, as a "Schedule I" drug, or one having a high potential for abuse and little known medical utility. Three-quarters of the states permit a maximum of six months incarceration for possession of 10 grams of marijuana (a typical retail amount) on first offense. (These data are from ImpacTeen Illicit Drug Team, *Illicit Drug Policies,* pp. 21, 28, and Section 4).

ciaries are felons, treatment is still not a politically favored remedy to the drug problem. There is reason to believe, though, that treatment's performance may improve in ways that are more obvious. Treatment modalities using depot naltrexone, immunotherapies and drug vaccines, buprenorphine, and contingency management hold promise. Developments such as these brighten the prospects for shifting addiction treatment into the medical mainstream. Should treatment quality improve, and should that improvement be successfully communicated to the public, its political support could increase as well.[11]
- Will political support for toughness among the public at large remain stable? It may not if credible options to the current regime are developed and publicized. Indeed, polls suggest that the public attitude toward drug policy is considerably more nuanced than are the statements of most politicians, at least at the federal level. Conventional wisdom holds that nuance does not play well on television and that hard-on-drugs sound bites are less risky than soft. Conceivably that could change, at least in some states.[12]
- Will racial and ethnic minorities remain divided on the question of toughness? Minorities offer about the same support for some aspects of drug law enforcement as whites do. However, there is also resentment over the number of minorities incarcerated on drug offenses and over laws limiting the availability of housing and other benefits to former drug offenders and their families. It is difficult to say how far such stresses can be pushed before they result in a collapse of minority support for antidrug efforts.[13]

How Might Less Predictable Developments Play?

We have discussed reasonably predictable drivers. The world is likely to evolve in less predictable ways, particularly in technological terms. We here offer a few plausible examples of low-probability developments with potentially high consequences for drug problems and policy.

- Developments in neuroscience. It is conceivable that a scientific breakthrough will result in a medication-based drug treatment protocol that is dramatically more effective

[11] For more on perceptions of addiction treatment and its limitations and promise, see McLellan et al., "Drug Dependence, a Chronic Medical Illness," and Leshner, "Science-Based Views of Drug Addiction and Its Treatment." On the public's impression: In 2001, 36 percent of adult Americans judged treatment "very effective" in controlling drugs, substantially fewer than the percentage applying that judgment to interdiction (52 percent) or domestic enforcement against sellers (49 percent) (Pew Research Center for the People & the Press, "Interdiction and Incarceration Still Top Remedies"). For the value of promising treatment modalities, see, for example, Comer et al., "Depot Naltrexone," and Griffith et al., "Contingency Management in Outpatient Methadone Treatment." On substance abuse treatment by physicians, see Merrill, "Integrating Medical Care and Addiction Treatment."

[12] Regarding the flexibility of the electorate on drug issues, about half of adult Americans believe mandatory minimum sentences should be rolled back, about half believe possession of small amounts of marijuana should be decriminalized, and three-quarters support permitting doctors to prescribe it (Pew Research Center for the People & the Press, "Interdiction and Incarceration Still Top Remedies"). For the political riskiness of appearing soft on drugs, see, for example, Bertram et al., *Drug War Politics,* pp. 162–168.

[13] Blacks are almost as likely as whites to agree that possession of small amounts of marijuana should be treated as a crime and to disagree that too many people are incarcerated for possession only (Pew Research Center for the People & the Press, "Interdiction and Incarceration Still Top Remedies").

at combating addiction than those currently employed or contemplated. If addiction is treatable, illicit drugs could become more attractive as intoxicants, and the policy focus could shift from addiction to intoxication. It is also conceivable that scientific advances will be made or exploited by drug manufacturers, who might invent new drugs that will mimic the attractions of current ones without their dangers, at least in the short run.

- A celebrity incident. In the 1980s, Len Bias's death focused public attention on the perils of cocaine and may have convinced many people who would otherwise have tried cocaine not to do so. Ecstasy has been enjoying a reputation as a "soft drug" much the way cocaine did in the 1970s. An overdose death of a celebrity, such as a pop star from a club drug, could change that, possibly with significant effect on initiation. Conversely, an equally well-known individual (or his or her child) could suffer grievous harm from enforcement action against what proved to be minor drug offenses. In such a case, public support for a more nuanced drug policy could crystallize in a way that politicians could not ignore.[14]
- Technological progress in drug testing. A means of testing may be developed that is cheap, quick, and not as intrusive as urine sampling. What if, for example, the presence of drugs could be determined through a patch placed on the arm for a few minutes? What if the patch simultaneously tested for other health indicators? Such a diagnostic tool might prove difficult for parents to resist. It might also break down some of the resistance on privacy grounds to widespread drug testing. This could affect not only drug use, but also drug policy inasmuch as it shifted some sanctioning activity from the criminal justice system to parents and other screeners.

What Implications Does the Future Have for the Present?

Policy formulation could only benefit from more attention to the future. In particular, predicting what would otherwise be unpleasant surprises could be helpful by focusing attention on elements of drug policy or other influences that, if addressed now, could reduce the chances of an unwanted turn of events. For example, one might favor greater investment in prevention today if one anticipates a future epidemic of some new drug than if one expects just a slow decay to endemic levels of the current drugs.

The value of futures analysis, however, is not limited to the avoidance of unpleasant surprises. By playing out specific scenarios to their ultimate consequences, policymakers could also identify complex issues whose eventual resolution could benefit from immediate attention. For instance, predictions of coming conflict between state and federal laws suggest initiating now a comprehensive discussion of federalism vis-á-vis drug policy, rather than doing so piecemeal as aspects of this issue are raised in the courts.

More generally, everyone may be better off in the long run if the time devoted to analyzing past trends and the current situation were supplemented by more anticipation of the future than has been the norm until now.

---

[14] On Len Bias, see Bennett, DiIulio, and Waters, *Body Count.* On ecstasy's reputation, see Cloud, "The Lure of Ecstasy." How Might U.S. Drug Problems and Policies Evolve?

CHAPTER SEVEN

How *Should* U.S. Drug Policies Evolve?

This paper aims to provide a source of information and analysis, not a detailed set of policy prescriptions. We believe, however, that there are some broad principles and some narrower directions that fall naturally out of an analytic perspective and the evidence so far brought to light. Some of these are not likely to draw strong value-oriented objections and are thus particularly amenable to serving as a starting point for consensus in this fractious domain. Others may be challenged by vested interests or observers with a particular moral perspective but seem to us to be pragmatically promising enough to warrant greater consideration than they have so far received. Let us begin with two broad principles whose acceptance seems to us essential if drug control policy is ever to be effective and if the debate over drug policy is to move beyond shrill advocacy of narrow, and thus only partial, "solutions." (Once again, it is worth noting that no one is in a position to mandate the adoption of these principles, although greater emphasis in federal rhetoric might well prove helpful.)

Manage This Long-Term Problem for the Long Term

As we have noted, America is not going to be the world's first drug-free society. No crash program or magic bullet will solve the drug problem. Instead, it is a problem that must be *managed* so as to limit the number of people who use, the frequency or duration of their use, and the damage they do to themselves and others, together with the damage resulting from policy choices. And it is important that, in choosing strategies to address this serious problem, we consider the costs and benefits accruing beyond the next two or four years.

Use All Policy Levers

This may seem too obvious to state, but we are not arguing here for rough equality of effort over enforcement, treatment, and prevention in all situations and on all occasions. We mean, rather, that all approaches be considered in formulating the policy mix to address the most pressing problems. Two generic guidelines are relevant here.

Time the Mix of Control Strategies to the Epidemic Cycle

In particular, the allocation of effort across strategies should vary as use of a drug progresses through the "epidemic cycle." As discussed above, in a drug epidemic, initial low levels of use give way to explosive (contagious) spread, which peaks and then falls back to some endemic level.

During the explosive growth stage, policy ought to do anything and everything possible to delay or diffuse the contagion resulting from personally communicated rosy information about the drug. Pragmatically, enforcement is the tool most capable of having a quick effect, so enforcement plays a uniquely valuable role. Enforcement, of course, is also a convenient rubric for a mélange of strategies whose suitability also varies with the situation. Early in an epidemic, it may be wisest to emphasize "buy-bust" stings that make retailers cautious about selling to strangers, along with wholesale interdiction that can create spot shortages. It makes less sense to commit resources to very long sentences, whose incapacitative effects may extend beyond the time of crisis.[1]

Later in the epidemic cycle, after initiation has dropped, there is less value in deterring new users, keeping prices high, or seeking to constrain supply. There are more heavy users who are generating substantial social costs, so it makes sense to invest relatively more in treatment than was the case during the explosive-growth stage. Treatment includes efforts both to curtail consumption by dependent users and to mitigate the adverse consequences of continued use.[2]

Prevention programs should always be under way. Because of its long lead times, prevention cannot be timed relative to an ongoing epidemic and, because its effects are generic across substances, it might help in slowing the outbreak of the next one, whenever that might be.[3]

Different drugs can be at different points in their epidemic cycles in the same year. For example, cocaine is now in the endemic stage; ecstasy use appears to have been growing explosively (see Figure 7.1). Thus, resources need not necessarily flow from enforcement to treatment and back again. It may be more a case of directing resources to specific drugs, for example, some of the enforcement resources previously devoted to cocaine might now be turned to ecstasy.[4]

Use the Right Tools for the Job

Aside from timing relative to epidemic stage, it is important to realize the distinctive values and limitations of each strategy so that each is brought to bear to the extent necessary but expectations stay in line with reality. Enforcement, for example, can serve well two important roles. First, it can make prohibition "real" by forcing market participants to "keep their heads

---

[1] See Caulkins, *Should the U.S. Direct More Law Enforcement Effort at XTC?*

[2] Behrens et al., "Optimal Control of Drug Epidemics: Prevent and Treat—But Not at the Same Time?"

[3] Caulkins et al., *An Ounce of Prevention, a Pound of Uncertainty*, pp. 56–57, 86–87.

[4] Caulkins, *Should the U.S. Direct More Law Enforcement Effort at XTC?*

Figure 7.1
Ecstasy Initiation Has Been Growing Explosively

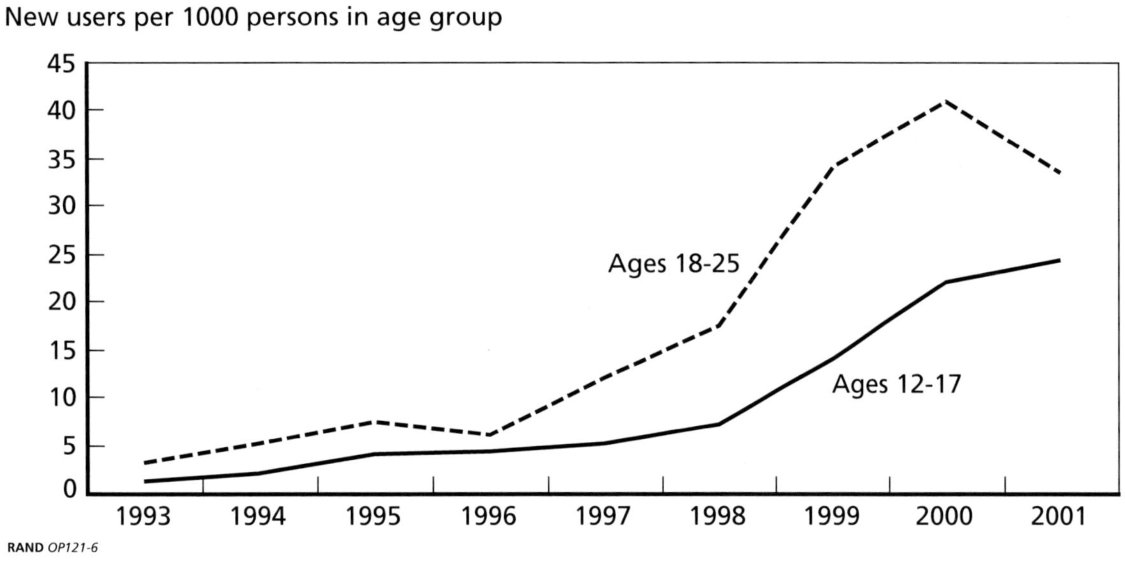

SOURCE: SAMHSA, "2003 National Survey of Drug Use and Health: Detailed Tables," Table 4.8A, http://oas.samhsa.gov/nhsda/2k3tabs/PDF/Sect4peTabs1to14.pdf. The two age groups shown account for most of the initiation. The total number of new ecstasy users across all age groups in 2001 was approximately 1.8 million, up from 200,000 in 1993.

down." Prohibition without enforcement invites greater drug use and harmful consequences. Second, enforcement can mold or shape the market into less destructive forms, even if it does not reduce the market's absolute size. For example, enforcement can drive public markets into covert forms of operation, such as beeper sales.[5]

Heightened enforcement has its limits. It is relatively ineffective at suppressing the quantity of drug consumed, and the associated crime and violence, for an established, mass-market drug. The reasons, discussed earlier, are largely the result of diffuse markets and easily replaced sellers. For established drugs, enforcement is generically subject to diminishing returns. That is, the next million dollars spent on enforcement buys less of a drop in drug consumption than the previous million spent. (Better returns are possible if the objective is not to decrease overall drug consumption but to displace local markets to other locations or forms.) Drug offense incarcerations have increased 15-fold over the last 20 years; at some time during that expansion, the point of diminishing returns must have been crossed. Thus, while more enforcement may have looked good 20 years ago, it makes less sense now.[6]

---

[5] On enforcement as a market-shaping device, see Kleiman, *Against Excess,* pp. 149–150.

[6] In 1979, 15,539 of 274,564 state prison inmates (5.7 percent) and 5,659 of 22,201 federal prison inmates (25.5 percent) had been convicted on drug charges. By 2000, those numbers had grown to 251,100 of 1,206,400 state inmates (20.8 percent) and 73,389 of 129,329 federal inmates (56.7 percent). Data are from Brown, Flanagan, and McLeod, *Sourcebook of Criminal Justice Statistics 1983,* p. 577; Flanagan, van Alstyne, and Gottfredson, *Sourcebook of Criminal Justice Statistics 1981,* p. 490; and Harrison and Beck, *Prisoners in 2001,* pp. 12–14.

Neither can much be expected of programs outside U.S. borders, which have had little effect on U.S. drug problems. Crop eradication and substitution, in particular, show minimal promise. Close to the drug source, costs are so low that enforcement-induced increases are likely to have no observable effect on street prices. The same is true of increases in the cost of land and labor for producing coca or opium. Obviously, there are many potentially valid reasons for intervention; those might include problems in the country that are partly caused by U.S. drug consumption. However, it is not credible to justify an intervention principally on the grounds that it will reduce U.S. drug consumption.[7]

In contrast to enforcement, treatment can cost-effectively reduce the consumption of an endemic drug and thus also reduce the harms associated with use. Thus, if the intent is to protect law-abiding taxpayers from drug-related crime, treatment is a cost-effective way of doing so. Treatment is cost-effective because the social costs of untreated use are enormous, but its scope is limited by the high rates of posttreatment relapse and by the practical difficulty of running heavy users through treatment numerous times to take advantage of their in-treatment use reductions. Obviously, a premium should be placed on developing new treatment methodologies (pharmacotherapeutic and otherwise). Research and development (R&D) is relatively inexpensive and could yield large returns on investments. Aside from its value to nonusers, treatment does more good to current users than either enforcement or prevention. Different people will judge that value as of more or less worth. Some people may not attach any worth to what they may see as aid to transgressors of the law, or they may prefer aiding individuals who have not broken the law. Others may take a more tolerant view, particularly in view of a growing body of research suggesting that drug addiction is not a matter of choice but of compulsion.[8]

Of the three principal approaches to drug control, prevention is the only one that attempts to address the problem before someone gets hurt. There is little doubt that prevention saves society more money than it costs, and its cost-effectiveness at reducing drug consumption is competitive with that of some enforcement strategies. Prevention, however, is cost-effective in no small part because it is inexpensive, not because it works like a vaccine. Prevention programs should continue, but they should not be expected to make a big difference in the nation's drug consumption. (Proponents of legalization hope that if money saved on enforcement were spent on prevention, much of the gain in use expected because of lower prices would be averted. That is expecting too much of prevention.)[9]

The strategies need not be viewed as alternatives, however. Enforcement and treatment, for example, can work together; in fact, as we have pointed out, they do work together, already. This cooperation, however, can be made more explicit and purposeful. Drug courts and other forms of coerced treatment use potential enforcement sanctions as an incentive to keep clients enrolled in treatment programs. A variant, termed "coerced abstinence," would require probationers or parolees to test negative for drugs or face imprisonment. How the offenders stayed clean would be up to them, but presumably, many would try treatment.[10]

---

[7] On crop eradication and substitution, see Riley, *Snow Job?* pp. 111–131.

[8] On the compulsive nature of addiction, see Leshner, "Science-Based Views of Drug Addiction and Its Treatment."

[9] Caulkins et al., *School-Based Drug Prevention,* pp. 26, 35; Caulkins et al., *An Ounce of Prevention, a Pound of Uncertainty,* pp. 52–53, 74–75, 78–79.

[10] Longshore et al., "Drug Courts." On coerced abstinence, see Kleiman, "Coerced Abstinence."

Draw Strength from Cross-State Variations in Drug Policy

As we have said, there is not a great deal of variation across states in drug policy—not nearly as much as there is between the United States and other countries. However, there is some. Within the generally prohibitionist regime, penalties vary substantially. For example, the statutory minimum prison term for possession of any amount of cocaine is 6 months in Ohio and Texas, but 3 years in New Jersey. A few states, for example, California, mandate treatment instead of incarceration for certain individuals convicted of drug use or possession. Many states make allowances for the medical use of marijuana, while almost as many do not. Among states that do, the scope and practical effect of the allowances vary substantially.[11]

Some state policies conflict with the federal approach. Not surprisingly, as it has in other domains in which it has claimed primacy, the federal government has sought to bring states into line with federal policy, through means ranging from jawboning to executive orders and litigation. We wonder whether both federal and state policy might benefit from a more flexible federal response. While continuing to challenge egregious departures from national policy, the federal government might seek to learn from state variations that do not seriously undermine the intent of the federal strategy.[12]

What effect such tolerable variations have in practice is unknown. There has been minimal effort to measure the effectiveness of different approaches to drug control within an enforcement-oriented regime. Perhaps equally as important, little is known as to whether laws that appear equally strict across states are actually enforced to varying degrees, either from state to state or from one jurisdiction to another within a state. Finally, little is known about how variations in the laws and enforcement practices affect behavior, including drug use, the crime and disorder associated with drug markets, and drug-related consequences. Do people even recognize that they live within a stricter or more lenient jurisdiction? Under a flexible approach, a strong emphasis would be placed on federally funded studies and data collection that would allow for evaluation of policy impact.

Evaluation of open questions and issues regarding variations within the prohibitionist regime might illuminate profitable directions for national and state policy. If by following one approach or another, some states were making more headway against drug use and its associated harms, it is difficult to see how anyone would be worse off by knowing that. It is easy to imagine that policy formulation and the associated debate might be moved toward more productive development than the current less-informed polemics can support. In this context, the federal government might even welcome cross-state variations in drug control policy that it viewed as falling within the broad scope of the national strategy.

---

[11] Penalties are from ImpacTeen Illicit Drug Team, *Illicit Drug Policies: Selected Laws from the 50 States,* pp. 91, 101, 117. On mandatory diversion in California, see Riley et al., "Drug Offenders and the Criminal Justice System." On medical marijuana, see Pacula et al., "State Medical Marijuana Laws."

[12] As an example of jawboning, the George W. Bush administration was reported to have lobbied Vermont's legislature and governor to reject the state's recent medical marijuana statute (Allen, "State Will Legalize Medical Marijuana Use"). Examples

Press for a More Dispassionate Debate

To conclude, we return to the spirit of our first two guidelines and offer another that is in the same vein but is not so much a policy suggestion as a suggestion for how to make policy. Even granted that drug policy is influenced by emotionally laden values, the debate has been remarkably polemical. And it is not just advocates of extreme positions or politicians currying favor with voters who have had recourse to sloganeering and sentiment. The public should ask that all parties to the debate concede the obvious: that children are important in our society and that freely available psychoactive drugs pose dangers to them. That established, the public should demand that the parties attend to the apparent or likely effects of current or alternative policies on children and other Americans. They should demand as much information on effects as they are now getting on the policies' consistency with the moral scruples of the discussants. Moral preferences can conflict, and when they do, there is not always an easy compromise to be made. For people who subscribe both to values suggesting strong prohibition and to values more consistent with alternative approaches, knowing which policies are most effective at alleviating the drug problem could be an important aid in decision making.

Further Reading

For further information on the topics summarized here, and for a range of well-expressed viewpoints, readers should find the following helpful.

Bertram, Eva, Morris Blachman, Kenneth Sharpe, and Peter Andreas, *Drug War Politics: The Price of Denial*, Berkeley: University of California Press, 1996.

Kleiman, Mark A. R., *Against Excess: Drug Policy for Results*, New York: Basic Books, 1992.

MacCoun, Robert J., and Peter Reuter, *Drug War Heresies: Learning from Other Vices, Times, and Places*, Cambridge, UK: Cambridge University Press, 2001.

Manski, Charles F., John V. Pepper, and Carol V. Petrie, eds., *Informing America's Policy on Illegal Drugs: What We Don't Know Keeps Hurting Us*, Washington, D.C.: National Academy Press, 2001, http://books.nap.edu/books/0309072735/html/index.html.

Musto, David F., *The American Disease: Origins of Narcotic Control*, 3rd ed., New York: Oxford University Press, 1999.

The White House, National *Drug Control Strategy*, Office of National Drug Control Policy, Washington, D.C., March 2004, http://www.whitehousedrugpolicy.gov/publications/policy/ndcs04/index.html.

Bibliography

Abt Associates, Inc. (William Rhodes, Mary Layne, Patrick Johnston, and Lynne Hozik), *What America's Users Spend on Illegal Drugs, 1988–1998* [NCJ 187080], Office of National Drug Control Policy, December 2000.

———, *What America's Users Spend on Illegal Drugs, 1988–2000,* NCJ 192334, Office of National Drug Control Policy, Washington, D.C., December 2001.

Allen, Darren M., "State Will Legalize Medical Marijuana Use," *The Barre Montpelier Times Argus,* May 20, 2004, The Media Awareness Project, http://www.mapinc.org/newscsdp/v04/n754/a10.html.

Anthony, James C., Lynn A. Warner, and Ronald C. Kessler, "Comparative Epidemiology of Dependence on Tobacco, Alcohol, Controlled Substances, and Inhalants: Basic Findings from the National Comorbidity Study," *Experimental and Clinical Psychopharmacology,* Vol. 2, No. 3, August 1994, pp. 244–268.

Behrens, Doris A., Jonathan P. Caulkins, Gernot Tragler, and Gustav Feichtinger, "Optimal Control of Drug Epidemics: Prevent and Treat—But Not at the Same Time?" *Management Science,* Vol. 46, No. 3, March 2000, pp. 333–347.

Bennett, William J., John J. DeIulio, Jr., and John P. Walters, *Body Count: Moral Poverty ... And How to Win America's War Against Crime and Drugs,* New York: Simon & Schuster, 1996.

Benson, Bruce L., and David W. Rasmussen, "The Context of Drug Policy: An Economic Interpretation," *Journal of Drug Issues,* Vol. 28, No. 3, Summer 1998, pp. 681–699.

Bertram, Eva, Morris Blachman, Kenneth Sharpe, and Peter Andreas, *Drug War Politics: The Price of Denial,* Berkeley: University of California Press, 1996.

Blumstein, Alfred, and Joan Petersilia, "Investing in Criminal Justice Research," in James Q. Wilson and Joan Petersilia, eds., *Crime,* San Francisco, Calif.: ICS Press, 1995, pp. 465–487.

Botvin, Gilbert J., "Principles of Prevention," in Robert M. Coombs and Douglas M. Ziedonis, eds., *Handbook of Drug Abuse Prevention: A Comprehensive Strategy to Prevent the Use of Alcohol and Other Drugs,* Boston: Allyn and Bacon, 1995, pp. 19–44.

Brown, Edward J., Timothy J. Flanagan, and Marueen McLeod, eds., *Sourcebook of Criminal Justice Statistics 1983,* Bureau of Justice Statistics, Washington, D.C., 1984.

Brownsberger, William N., "Prevalence of Frequent Cocaine Use in Urban Poverty Areas," *Contemporary Drug Problems,* Vol. 24, Summer 1997, pp. 349–371.

Caulkins, Jonathan P., "Modeling the Domestic Distribution Network for Illicit Drugs," *Management Science,* Vol. 43, No. 10, October 1997, pp. 1364–1371.

———, "Measurement and Analysis of Drug Problems and Drug Control Efforts," in David Duffee, ed., *Measurement and Analysis of Crime and Justice,* Vol. 4 of *Criminal Justice 2000,* NCJ 182411, National Institute of Justice, Washington, D.C., July 2000, pp. 391–449.

———, *Should the U.S. Direct More Law Enforcement Effort at XTC?* CT-171, Santa Monica, Calif.: RAND Corporation, June 2000.

———, "Law Enforcement's Role in a Harm Reduction Regime," *Crime and Justice Bulletin* No. 64, New South Wales Bureau of Crime and Justice Research, 2002.

Caulkins, Jonathan P., Rosalie Liccardo Pacula, Susan Paddock, and James Chiesa, *School-Based Drug Prevention: What Kind of Drug Use Does It Prevent?* MR-1459-RWJ, Santa Monica, Calif.: RAND Corporation, 2002.

Caulkins, Jonathan P., C. Peter Rydell, William L. Schwabe, and James Chiesa, *Mandatory Minimum Drug Sentences: Throwing Away the Key or the Taxpayers' Money?* MR-827-DPRC, Santa Monica, Calif.: RAND Corporation, 1997.

Caulkins, Jonathan P., C. Peter Rydell, Susan S. Everingham, James R. Chiesa, Shawn Bushway, *An Ounce of Prevention, a Pound of Uncertainty,* MR-923-RWJ, Santa Monica, Calif.: RAND Corporation, 1999.

Cloud, John, "The Lure of Ecstasy," *Time,* Vol. 155, No. 23, June 5, 2000, pp.62–68.

Comer, Sandra D., Eric D. Collins, Herbert D. Kleber, Elie S. Nuwayser, James H. Kerrigan, and Marian W. Fischman, "Depot Naltrexone: Long-Lasting Antagonism of the Effects of Heroin in Humans," *Psychopharmacology,* Vol. 159, No. 4, February 2002, pp. 351–360.

Congressional Record—Senate, Vol. 147, No. 167, S12439, December 5, 2001.

Courtwright, David T., "Which Sides Are You On?: Religion, Sexuality, and Culture-War Politics" (working title), in Mark Carnes, ed. New York: Columbia University Press, forthcoming.

———, *Forces of Habit: Drugs and the Making of the Modern World,* Cambridge, Mass.: Harvard University Press, 2001.

Crane, Barry D., A. Rex Rivolo, and Gary C. Comfort, *An Empirical Examination of Counterdrug Interdiction Program Effectiveness,* P-3219, Institute for Defense Analyses, January 1997.

Cussen, Meaghan, and Walter Block, "Legalize Drugs Now!: An Analysis of the Benefits of Legalized Drugs," *American Journal of Economics and Sociology,* Vol. 59, No. 3, July 2000. pp. 525–536.

Drug Policy Alliance, "Outgoing Drug Czar Issues Report Claiming 'Substantial Progress'; Critics Say Drug War Has Failed, New Standards Are Needed," *Drug Policy News,* January 4, 2001, http://www.drugpolicy.org/news/pressroom/pressrelease/pr_january04_01xczar.cfm.

Duhamel, Louise M., "Drug Use Outcomes in Four Substance Abuse Treatment Studies," Fact Sheet 29, National Evaluation Data Services, January 2000.

Ehisen, Rich, "States Keep Medical Marijuana Debate Alive," *State Net Capitol News,* Vol. XI, No. 19, May 12, 2003.

European Monitoring Centre for Drugs and Drug Abuse, *Annual Report 2003: The State of the Drugs Problem in the European Union and Norway,* Statistical Table 1, http://www.emcdda.eu.int/pdfs/stattab01-en/pdf.

Everingham, Susan S., and C. Peter Rydell, *Modeling the Demand for Cocaine,* MR-332-ONDCP/A/DPRC, Santa Monica, Calif.: RAND Corporation, 1994.

Federal Bureau of Investigation, *Crime in the United States, 2001: Uniform Crime Reports,* U.S. Department of Justice, Washington, D.C., October 28, 2002.

Fellner, Jamie, Marc Mauer, and Paul Hirschfield, "Losing the Vote: the Impact of Felony Disenfranchisement Laws in the United States," The Sentencing Project and Human Rights Watch, 1998, http://www.sentencingproject.org/pdfs/9080.pdf.

Flanagan, Timothy J., David J. van Alstyne, and Michael R. Gottfredson, *Sourcebook of Criminal Justice Statistics 1981,* Bureau of Justice Statistics, Washington, D.C., 1982.

Golub, Andrew, and Bruce D. Johnson, "Variation in Youthful Risks of Progression from Alcohol and Tobacco to Marijuana and to Hard Drugs Across Generations," *American Journal of Public Health,* Vol. 91, No. 2, February 2001, pp. 225–32.

Greenhouse, Linda, "States Rights Defense Falters in Medical Marijuana Case," *New York Times,* November 30, 2004, p. A20.

Griffith, James D., Grace A. Rowan-Szal, Ryan R. Roark, and D. Dwayne Simpson, "Contingency Management in Outpatient Methadone Treatment: A Meta-Analysis," *Drug and Alcohol Dependence,* Vol. 58, Nos. 1–2, February 1, 2000, pp. 55–66.

Haaga, J., and P. Reuter, "The Limits of the Czar's Ukase: Drug Policy at the Local Level," *Yale Law & Policy Review,* Vol. 8, No. 1, 1990, pp. 36–74.

Harrison, Paige M., and Allen J. Beck, *Prisoners in 2001,* Bureau of Justice Statistics, Washington, D.C., July 2002.

Hoffman, David, *Who Pays the Federal Individual Income Tax?* Special Report No. 118, Tax Foundation, Washington, D.C., November 2002.

Hser, Yih-ing, Valerie Hoffman, Christine E. Grella, and M. Douglas Anglin, "A 33-Year Follow-Up of Narcotics Addicts," *Archives of General Psychiatry,* Volume 58, May 2001, pp. 503–508.

Iguchi, Martin Y., Jennifer A. London, Nell Griffith Forge, Laura Hickman, Terry Fain, and Kara Riehman, "Elements of Well-Being Affected by Criminalizing the Drug User," *Public Health Reports,* Vol. 117, Supp. 1, 2002, pp. S146–S150.

ImpacTeen Illicit Drug Team, *Illicit Drug Policies: Selected Laws from the 50 States,* Berrien Springs, Mich.: Andrews University, 2002.

Internal Revenue Service, "Tax Stats at a Glance," http://www.irs.gov/taxstats/article/0,,id = 102886,00.html.

Johnston, Lloyd D., Patrick M. O'Malley, and Jerald G. Bachman, *Monitoring the Future: National Survey Results on Drug Use, 1975–2002, Volume I: Secondary School Students,* NIH Publication No. 03-5375, Bethesda, Md.: National Institute on Drug Abuse, 2003.

Kandel, Denise, Kevin Chen, Lynn A. Warner, Ronald C. Kessler, and Bridget Grant, "Prevalence and Demographic Correlates of Symptoms of Last Year Dependence on Alcohol, Nicotine, Marijuana, and Cocaine in the U.S. Population," *Drug and Alcohol Dependence,* Vol. 44, No. 1, January 10, 1997, pp. 11–29.

Kleiman, Mark A. R., *Against Excess: Drug Policy for Results*, New York: Basic Books, 1992.

———, "Coerced Abstinence: A Neopaternalist Drug Policy Initiative," in Lawrence M. Mead, ed., *The New Paternalism: Supervisory Approaches to Poverty,* Washington, D.C.: Brookings Institution, 1997, pp. 182–219.

———, "The Problem of Replacement and the Logic of Drug Law Enforcement," *Drug Policy Analysis Bulletin,* No. 3, 1997.

Knoll, Claudia, and Doris Zuba, *Modeling the U.S. Cocaine Epidemic: Dynamic Trajectories of Initiation and Demand,* master's thesis, Technical University of Vienna, 2002.

Leshner, Alan I., "Science-Based Views of Drug Addiction and Its Treatment," *Journal of the American Medical Association,* Vol. 282, No. 14, October 13, 1999, pp. 1314–1316.

LexisNexis, "Public Opinion Online," April 19, 2002. Reported by Roper Center at the University of Connecticut, http://web.lexis-nexis.com/universe (as of April 19, 2002, and November 18, 2004).

Longshore, Douglas, Susan Turner, Suzanne Wenzel, Andrew Morral, Adele Harrell, Duane McBride, Elizabeth Deschenes, and Martin Iguchi, "Drug Courts: A Conceptual Framework," *Journal of Drug Issues,* Vol. 31, No. 1, Winter 2001, pp. 7–26.

Lynskey, M.T., A.C. Heath, K.K. Bucholz, W.S. Slutske, P.A. Madden, E.C. Nelson, D.J. Statham, and N.G. Martin, "Escalation of Drug Use in Early-Onset Cannabis Users vs. Co-Twin Controls," *Journal of the American Medical Association,* Vol. 289, No. 4, January 22, 2003, pp. 427–433.

MacCoun, Robert J., and Peter Reuter, *Drug War Heresies: Learning from Other Vices, Times, and Places,* Cambridge, UK: Cambridge University Press, 2001.

Maguire, Kathleen, and Ann L. Pastore, *Sourcebook of Criminal Justice Statistics 1999,* Bureau of Justice Statistics, Washington, D.C.: U.S. Government Printing Office, 2000.

Maguire, Kathleen, and Ann L. Pastore, *Sourcebook of Criminal Justice Statistics 2000,* Bureau of Justice Statistics, Washington, D.C.: U.S. Government Printing Office, 2001.

Manski, Charles F., John V. Pepper, and Carol V. Petrie, eds., *Informing America's Policy on Illegal Drugs: What We Don't Know Keeps Hurting Us,* Washington, D.C.: National Academy Press, 2001, http://books.nap.edu/books/0309072735/html/index.html.

McLellan, A. Thomas, David C. Lewis, Charles P. O'Brien, and Herbert D. Kleber, "Drug Dependence, a Chronic Medical Illness: Implications for Treatment, Insurance, and Outcomes Evaluation," *Journal of the American Medical Association,* Vol. 284, No. 13, October 4, 2002, pp. 1689–1695.

Merrill, Joseph O., "Integrating Medical Care and Addiction Treatment," *Journal of General Internal Medicine,* Vol. 18, No. 1, 2003, pp. 68–69.

Morral, Andrew R., Daniel F. McCaffrey, and Susan M. Paddock, "Reassessing the Marijuana Gateway Effect," *Addiction,* Vol. 97, No. 12, December 2002, pp. 1493–1504.

Mumola, Christopher J., *Incarcerated Parents and Their Children,* NCJ 182335, Bureau of Justice Statistics, Washington, D.C., August 2000.

Murphy, Patrick, Lynn E. Davis, Timothy Liston, David Thaler, and Kathi Webb, *Improving Anti-Drug Budgeting,* MR-1262-ONDCP/NSF, Santa Monica, Calif.: RAND Corporation, 2000.

Musto, David F., "Lessons of the First Cocaine Epidemic," *The Wall Street Journal,* June 11, 1986, p. 30.

———, *The American Disease: Origins of Narcotic Control,* 3rd ed., New York: Oxford University Press, 1999.

The National Center for Health Statistics, *Health, United States, 2002.*

The National Center on Addiction and Substance Abuse at Columbia University, *Cigarettes, Alcohol, Marijuana: Gateways to Illicit Drug Use, Introduction*, New York: National Center on Addiction and Substance Abuse at Columbia University, October 1994.

The National Institute of Justice, *2000 Arrestee Drug Abuse Monitoring: Annual Report,* NCJ 193013, U.S. Department of Justice, Washington, D.C., April 2003.

The National Institute on Drug Abuse, "NIDA InfoFacts: Drug Abuse and AIDS," http://www.nida.nih.gov/Infofax/DrugAbuse.html.

———, "NIDA Community Drug Alert Bulletin—Hepatitis," May 2000, http://www.drugabuse.gov/HepatitisAlert/HepatitisAlert.html.

Pacula, Rosalie Liccardo, Jamie F. Chriqui, Deborah A. Reichmann, and Yvonne M. Terry-MacElrath, "State Medical Marijuana Laws: Understanding the Laws and Their Limitations," *Journal of Public Health Policy,* Vol. 23, No. 4, 2002, pp. 413–439.

Pew Research Center for the People & the Press, "Interdiction and Incarceration Are Still Top Remedies," March 21, 2001, http://people-press.org/reports/display.php3?ReportID=16.

President, Proclamation, "Proclamation 7470—Family Day, 2001," Weekly Compilation of Presidential Statements, Washington, D.C., September 24, 2001.

Reuter, Peter, "Why Can't We Make Prohibition Work Better?: Some Consequences of Ignoring the Unattractive," *Proceedings of the American Philosophical Society,* Vol. 141, No. 3, September 1997, pp. 262–275.

———, "The Limits of Supply-Side Drug Control," *The Milken Institute Review,* First Quarter, 2001, pp. 14–23.

———, "Why Does Research Have So Little Impact on American Drug Policy?" *Addiction,* Vol. 96, 2001, pp. 373–376.

Reuter, Peter, Gordon Crawford, and Jonathan Cave, *Sealing the Borders: The Effects of Increased Military Participation in Drug Intervention,* R-3594-USDP, Santa Monica, Calif.: RAND Corporation, 1988.

Riley, Kevin Jack, Patricia A. Ebener, James Chiesa, Susan Turner, and Jeanne S. Ringel, *Drug Offenders and the Criminal Justice System: Will Proposition 36 Treat or Create Problems?* IP-204, Santa Monica, Calif.: RAND Corporation, 2002.

Riley, Kevin Jack, *Snow Job?: The War Against International Cocaine Trafficking,* New Brunswick, N.J.: Transaction Publishers, 1996.

Rydell, C. Peter, and Susan S. Everingham, *Controlling Cocaine: Supply Versus Demand Programs,* MR-331-ONDCP/A/DPRC, Santa Monica, Calif.: RAND Corporation, 1994.

Saffer, Henry, and Frank Chaloupka, "The Demand for Illicit Drugs," *Economic Inquiry,* Vol. 37, No. 3, July 1999, pp. 401–411.

Stares, Paul B., *Global Habit: The Drug Problem in a Borderless World,* Washington, D.C.: Brookings Institution, 1996.

Substance Abuse and Mental Health Services Administration (SAMHSA), Office of Applied Studies, *2002 National Survey on Drug Use & Health: Detailed Tables.*

Substance Abuse and Mental Health Services Administration (SAMHSA), Office of Applied Studies, *2003 National Survey on Drug Use & Health: Detailed Tables,* http://oas.samhsa.gov/nhsda/2k3tabs/PDF/Sect7peTabs1to12.pdf.

———, Office of Applied Studies, "Detailed Tables for 1999 and 2000 National Household Surveys on Drug Abuse."

———, Office of Applied Studies, *Drug Abuse Warning Network,* 2002.

———, Office of Applied Studies, "Results from the 2001 National Household Survey on Drug Abuse: Volume III. Detailed Tables."

———, Office of Applied Studies. *Treatment Episode Data Set (TEDS): 1992–2001. National Admissions to Substance Abuse Treatment Services,* DASIS Series: S-20, DHHS Publication No. (SMA) 03-3778, Rockville, MD, 2003.

Sullivan, Terry, "Missouri Sentencing Changes Stem Need for Prison Growth," *Corrections Journal,* June 9, 2003, pp. 1–2.

Tonry, Michael, *Malign Neglect: Race, Crime, and Punishment in America,* Oxford, UK: Oxford University Press, 1995.

Tragler, Gernot, Jonathan P. Caulkins, and Gustav Feichtinger, "Optimal Dynamic Allocation of Treatment and Enforcement in Illicit Drug Control," *Operations Research,* Vol. 49, No. 3, May–June 2001, pp. 352–362.

University of Michigan, "Monitoring the Future: 2003 Data from In-School Surveys of 8th-, 10th-, and 12th-Grade Students," http://www.monitoringthefuture.org/data/03data.html#2003data-drugs.

U.S. Customs Service—America's Frontline: Performance and Annual Report Fiscal Year 2002.

U.S. Department of Agriculture, Commodity and Marketing Programs, "U.S. General Imports of Agricultural, Fish, and Forestry Products from Colombia," 1997–2001.

Vanyukov, M. M., and R. E. Tarter, "Genetic Studies of Substance Abuse," *Drug and Alcohol Dependence,* Vol. 59, No. 2, May 1, 2000, pp. 101–123.

Vlahov, David, Don C. Des Jarlais, Eric Goosby, Paula C. Hollinger, Peter G. Lurie, Michael D. Shriver, and Steffanie Strathdee, "Needle Exchange Programs for the Prevention of Human Immunodeficiency Virus Infection: Epidemiology and Policy," *American Journal of Epidemiology,* supplement to Vol. 154, No. 12, December 15, 2001, pp. S70–S77.

Wagner, Fernando A., and James C. Anthony, "Into the World of Illegal Drug Use: Exposure Opportunity and Other Mechanisms Linking the Use of Alcohol, Tobacco, Marijuana, and Cocaine," *American Journal of Epidemiology,* Vol. 155, No. 10, 2002, pp. 918–925.

The White House, *National Drug Control Strategy,* Office of National Drug Control Policy, Washington, D.C., February 1989.

———, *The National Drug Control Strategy, 1996: Program, Resources, and Evaluation,* Office of National Drug Control Policy, Washington, D.C.

———, *The National Drug Control Strategy: 1999,* Office of National Drug Control Policy, Washington, D.C., 1999.

———, *National Drug Control Strategy,* Office of National Drug Control Policy, Washington, D.C., February 2002.

———, National *Drug Control Strategy,* Office of National Drug Control Policy, Washington, D.C., February 2003, http://www.whitehousedrugpolicy.gov/publications/policy/ndcs03/index.html.

———, *National Drug Control Strategy,* Office of National Drug Control Policy, Washington, D.C., March 2004.

Wilson, James Q., "What, if Anything, Can the Federal Government Do to Reduce Crime?" in *Perspectives on Crime and Justice: 1996–1997 Lecture Series,* Vol. 1, U.S. Department of Justice, November 1997, pp. 1–12.

Winkler, Doris, Jonathan P. Caulkins, Doris Behrens, and Gernot Tragler, "Estimating the Relative Efficiency of Various Forms of Prevention at Different Stages of a Drug Epidemic," *Socio-Economic Planning Sciences,* Vol. 38, No. 1, 2004, pp. 43–56.

Zielbauer, Paul von, "Rethinking the Key Thrown Away: As Ashcroft Cracks Down, States Cut Prison Terms," *New York Times,* September 28, 2003, p. 41.Bibliography